The Church in Bondage

Problems and Trends in The United Methodist Church

Allen O. Morris

Express Press, Lima, Ohio

THE CHURCH IN BONDAGE

FIRST EDITION
Copyright © 2000 by
Allen O. Morris

ISBN 0-7880-1600-8　　　　　　　　　PRINTED IN U.S.A.

Dedicated
To the revival
of the United
Methodist Church
in the United States

Table of Contents

Acknowledgements

I was having lunch with The Reverend Larry Eisenberg in Tulsa, Oklahoma when he interrupted me, pointed to me, and said, "The Lord told me that you need to write a book." His words echoed what I had been thinking over the previous year. That got this book "on the way."

I owe a debt of gratitude to so many people. First, my father Edward O. Morris who, even though he had to drop out of school in the fourth grade to go to work in the cotton and tobacco fields of South Georgia to support his family, was tough on us kids, but inspired us and never stopped learning himself; I have the highest degree of respect for him. My brother Smokey; we have been through a lot together. My family, who provided continuous learning opportunities. George Holst and J. G. Smith, Sr., principals of my junior and senior high schools respectively, took an interest in every one of "their kids" — that went beyond the campus. "J.G.", as we called him behind his back, engineered my receiving that all-important Trull Scholarship which paid for my first two years of college. I treasured Mr. & Mrs. Darius B. Rohrer, "Pops" and "Grandma", who absorbed me into their extended family and provided numerous adopted brothers, sisters, aunts, uncles, cousins, nieces, and nephews. Terri Metcalf Moore, my heart of hearts, is closer than any sister could be. Mrs. Pauline White is like a second mother to me. I thank all of the other people, to remain unnamed, who have helped me in so many ways.

The three other men, Jimmy Cash, Jr., John McCarthy, and Samuel Wood, Jr., who shared the same concerns with me and formed the nucleus of Concerned Methodists here in Fayetteville, North Carolina over eleven years ago, are to be recognized. Each one is talented in so many ways.

I especially appreciate all of the United Methodist pastors who refuse to compromise their integrity on the altar of "upward mobility" within the institutional church; they are combat veterans in the truest sense of the word. They will not fully realize all the good they have done until they reach heaven.

I appreciate so much the wonderful country in which we live, that provides the freedom and opportunity to become "all that we can be" — and then some.

Most of all, I am infinitely grateful to a merciful God Who is the reason I am here today. Otherwise, I would not have recovered from that "near death experience" I had in 1980. Five years later, He gave me a life-changing "Damascus Road" experience that opened my eyes to what it was to be a Christian (at age thirty-nine) and put me onto the road of serving Him. (This testimony is on the Concerned Methodists' website under "A Texas Mule")

It took a United Methodist evangelist, Barbara Brokhoff, to express the depth of gratitude I feel. She was at her hair-dresser's in Florida when he asked her in a somewhat cynical manner, "Jesus is just a crutch for you, isn't he?" She looked down, shook her head from side to side, laughed, and replied, "Oh no, He's not my crutch. You see, He is much more than that. Jesus Christ is my next breath."

You see, that is what He is to me: "Jesus Christ is my next breath."

Foreword

I was speaking to a congregation of people on a sweltering summer night at a United Methodist Church in South Georgia. I was about to conclude an evening session on issues facing our denomination and was pleased at how the evening had progressed. Even though I have a policy of welcoming all questions and challenges in a spirit of openness, the people had been cordial - reflective of the gracious courtesy common to those living in that part of the country.

Then, in the back, one man raised his hand to be recognized. After I called on him, in a loud voice he said , "I was raised an Episcopalian. Tell me, with all of the problems in the United Methodist Church, why should I stay?"

I thought to myself, "How can I answer that? Yes, how could I answer that question?...."

First Beginnings

When three other men and I met in 1988 to discuss concerns that we shared in our two United Methodist churches, little did we know to what extent our efforts would carry us. We had shared these concerns with our pastors. We believed that these clergy would discuss the issues with our bishop and the problems would be corrected. Not so. Instead, we were told in so many words that we were mistaken in our beliefs, did not have a grasp of the problems, should go along with those who "knew better," and were the only ones who shared the concerns.

We discussed it among ourselves and weighed what we had been told. First, all of us were certain of our perceptions because we had done our homework and knew that our data was reliable. Secondly, we had traveled through much of the world, had a solid base of experience, and were well-versed in the problem areas, sometimes having been personally involved in those parts of the world; some of us had worked at the highest levels in our professions and made significant contributions in our specialty areas. Third, we saw no reason to "just go along"; we could think for ourselves. Finally, we conceded that even if we were the only ones who had these concerns, we would do what we could to influence our denomination as much as possible.

We were happy to learn that we were wrong in two ways: 1. as soon as we "went public" with our information and our organization, we learned that we were not alone - there were hundreds of thousands of people who shared similar concerns; and 2. all of the clergy had not "sold out" their integrity to enhance their "upward mobility" within the system; there are many who stand firm for their faith - with integrity and often in the face of intimidating pressure.

Commitment to Truth

Sensing that the task of reforming our denomination would be too great for any group, much less the four of us, we based our efforts on four principles: lifting up our United Methodist Church in prayer; maintaining a strong relationship with the Lord; having a passion for the truth; and communicating as much information to as many people as possible. Chuck Swindoll states, "Being a loving Christian doesn't excuse us from reporting the hard thing. The river of love must be kept within its banks. Truth on one side, discernment on the other." (1)

Methodology

In problem solving, there are good secular models: for the scientist, there is the "Scientific Method"; for the doctor, there is the medical diagnosis; for the military man, there is the "Estimate of the Situation"; and for the business executive - corporate problem solving. Jesus has instructed us to "inspect fruit" (Matthew 7:15-23). All have in common observing facts, events, and symptoms; formulating different theories to explain what has been observed; deciding what is the most logical explanation, and then proposing solutions.

It must be observed that there are many good things happening in local churches; the problems tend to be in our institutional church. We proceed in the spirit of examining past actions and offering our view on where the Church is headed. I believe it was George

Santayana who said, "Those who do not remember history are doomed to repeat it."

We believe it necessary to do this so that we can face the problems; this sometimes painful first step is necessary if we are to reverse our over-30 year decline. It is also important to observe that people do not always operate from a base of sound logic and can be influenced by emotional appeals. Two principles effectively used by Dr. Paul Josef Goebbels and numerous others since he formulated them in the 1930s were:

1. A truth can be so big and unpleasant that people will refuse to believe it.

2. A lie can sound plausible and be repeated so often that it will be believed.

Looking to the Future

"We are convinced that The United Methodist Church faces a crisis unequaled to any since the schism preceding the Civil War. The continued membership decline is the major symptom of this crisis, but the issues are deeper and more complex than the loss of members. In any organization, when things are not going well, there are always those who urge silence, unquestioning loyalty, and the suppression of all criticism. But our church is too important to be allowed to wither if there is some means of giving it new life." (2)

We invite you to examine what has been written here. This is not so much a "this is the way it is" work, but more akin to an anthology of data prefaced by an extended series of observations and commentary. If it upsets you, we recommend you focus on the factuality of the information and who caused it to happen, not those of us who are the messengers. We have considered the history of the church over the past nineteen years; researched voluminous amounts of information; spoken with thousands of people from all walks of life; and correlated a multitude of factors together. We present what we have concluded, proffer theories as to the causes of our past decline, and offer what we see as the future of our denomination. Don't be surprised if a lot of this information comes as a surprise to you. We often say that the people in the pews are

13

unaware of over 99% of what happens in the United Methodist Church.

Caution!

To make this as clear as possible, we have included names, dates, and specific information as necessary. We believe this to be more beneficial than to write in nebulous terms such as "a bishop said" or "a laywoman did" in clarifying the very real problems of our church. This may not be enjoyable literature, but it is necessary; reading it may have all of the interest of a surgeon poring over a manual on how to excise malignant growths.

We ask that you would read what we have presented here with this background in mind, research the truth for yourself, and be assured of our love for the 8.4 million members who call themselves "United Methodist." You owe it to yourself, your children, and to the future of the United Methodist Church.

Notes:
1. "Letters of Reference" from *Come Before Winter* by Charles R. Swindoll; Multnomah Press, Portland, Oregon; 1985; page 201.
2. From the Preface to *Rekindling the Flame*, by Professor William H. Willimon and the late Professor Robert L. Wilson, 1987, p. 9. This book is available for reading on the Concerned Methodists website at http://www.cmpage.org

1

Julie+

Assume that you and I are in the same church. You are a married couple with a fifteen-year old daughter named Julie. Now, for the sake of this story, I am a youth counselor* in our church; Julie is one of "my" kids.

One day, we have a meeting at my request - the both of you, Julie's mother and father, and I, Julie's youth counselor. Gently, very gently, I share with you the fact that Julie has a problems with drugs: not just marijuana but also the "hard drugs" such as cocaine and heroin.

Now, your reaction would be understandable. You would be shocked and react with, "Julie? Our Julie? The girl that we raised from a baby? This beautiful girl whom we love so much? The girl who is so talented and has given us so much joy? This is the girl we will be sending to college in a few years! No, it can't be true!" This would be the normal reaction of any parents who love their girl. But what would be important, of crucial importance, is what you would do then.

If you persisted in this train of thought and refused to recognize the reality of her situation, then she would, in all probability, get worse. Her drug habit would cause her to crave ever increasing amounts; she would have to do things to get more and more money, such as stealing, or prostitution, or selling the drugs herself. In the process of stealing, prostituting herself, or selling the drugs, she would bring harm to herself and others. If she did not get help, the course of the addiction is that she would one day die from a drug overdose, violence, or possibly a debilitating disease such as AIDS.

Or, if you could overcome the initial shock, anger, and disappointment, and examine the situation objectively, you would realize that I loved Julie and even thought of her as my own daughter. You would remember that you had seen some of those same signs yourselves, but not wanted to admit them to yourselves because they might seem to tarnish your love for her. But if you want to truly help Julie, you must look dispassionately at the reality of the situation, admit its truthfulness, and then resolve to do whatever you could to try to get her out of the habit. Only in that way would you have any hope of seeing her restored to health and back on the track to a healthy, productive life.

You might resort to "tough love" by refusing to give her spending money; not allowing her to go on unsupervised recreational outings; and monitoring closely all areas of her life. As a result, she would react emotionally, saying that you "hate her" and "don't love her" and are being "mean-spirited."

This is analogous to the situation in which we find ourselves in our denomination. Julie, the beautiful teenager that you love so much, is our United Methodist Church. It has done so much good in the past and does so today; but it has some problems - serious, fundamental ones that pose a danger to the health, indeed, the future of our church. I am a messenger - the bearer of bad news. Some of you have known for many years the nature of our problems; others have not realized they were quite as serious as they are. Still other have been unaware that anything has been wrong.

+   This is purely a fictional girl with no relation to any real person.
*   I have served as both a Youth Coordinator and counselor for over 200 teenagers over the space of fourteen years in two different churches and one orphanage

Visible Problem Indicators

Just as in the situation with "Julie" - there are visible problems indicating that our United Methodist Church is in trouble.

One question we have heard on occasion is, "Why do you talk about our problems? Why don't you spend an equal amount of time talking about all the good that the church does?" First, there is an army of church employees and members who do exactly that; their efforts don't need to be reinforced by anyone else. Secondly, we can best explain this by the example of a doctor treating a patient with a malignant tumor. The actual number of cancerous cells is very small compared to the total number of healthy cells in the patient's body. But if the doctor were to spend a proportionate amount of time concentrating on the good cells as he did on the bad ones, his patient would die. Instead, he concentrates his full attention on the bad cells because he knows that if he doesn't, the bad cells will multiply, overwhelm the good cells, and ultimately destroy the body killing the patient.

It is for those same reasons that this book focuses on the problems in our denomination; if we cannot accurately diagnose the problems and implement an effective cure, the denomination may continue to shrink and ultimately die.

Membership Loss

The most visible problems indicating the decline of our United Methodist Church (UMC) is that of the continuing loss of members over the past twenty nine years - a total of 2,379,976. This is an average loss of 82,068 people per year, 6,839 per month, 1,579 per week, or 225.6 per day, for every one of those years. This is happening in a country with an increasing population and other, more evangelical denominations of a congregational nature that are also growing (Appendix A).

Closed Churches

In Danville, Virginia, the historical marker on the front of Calvary United Methodist Church reads, "Founded by 47 people on November 14, 1879. First organized religious group in North Danville. On Nov. 14, 1887, a new sanctuary was dedicated and known as Calvary Methodist Episcopal Church South." In 1998, another sign on the front read "For Sale". The irony is that across the road in this section of town is a Baptist church that has a thriving congregation.

During the past quarter of a century, a large number of our once large and vibrant urban congregations have either declined drastically or closed. A few examples will illustrate this trend: in 1960, the Barton Heights Church (Richmond, Virginia) had 1,031 members; Narden Park (Detroit, Michigan) had 2,401; and City Church (Gary, Indiana) had 1,687. Today none of these congregations exists. (1) Each physical structure that stands empty indicating a closed UM church is the accumulation of unfulfilled hopes and dreams, and - heartbreak.

This comes as no surprise when related to membership loss. From an unrelated study, we learned that the average size of a church in mainline denominations is 156 members. This means that we have had the equivalent of one United Methodist church closing its doors for every single day, seven days a week, 365 days a year, for the past twenty-nine years. We have a serious problem.

Notes: 1. *Rekindling the Flame*, p. 19.

Stewardship

"Whoever can be trusted with very little can also be trusted with much, and whoever is dishonest with very little will also be dishonest with much. So if you have not been trustworthy in handling worldly wealth, who will trust you with true riches?" Luke 16:10,11 (NIV)

"At the beginning of last year, I traveled to Jacksonville, Florida to respond to allegations made that our data in "The 1997 Steward-ship Report on the United Methodist Church" was "inaccurate and misleading." Mr. John Edgecombe, a Certified Public Accountant (CPA) who attends Lakewood UMC in that city, wrote an analysis of our information and I had been invited by Dr. Ernest Lott of that church to defend our figures. I carried thousands of pages of data that we had used in our analysis and met with the leadership of Lakewood Church. I invited the people to discuss our data with me if they had any problems with its accuracy; there were none. Even though Mr. Edgecombe was sitting in the congregation at the time, he did not say a word to me. The next day at church, I attempted to speak with him; when he saw me, he turned around and walked the other way. I caught up with him, introduced myself, and started to speak with him; he excused himself and walked away. He was willing to criticize our work when none of us were there to defend it; when I was, he would not engage me in discussion. I was eagerly looking forward to discussing with him the accuracy of our information and that of the document he had published to rebut ours: "Apportionments - A Review of the Issues." An open public debate would, and will, reveal what is the truth.

This is a recurring situation in our denomination. We research the data before we disseminate it and invite others to challenge its accuracy - with a willingness to correct de facto errors. Instead, what we find is that some people will make allegations in our absence of its being "inaccurate and misleading" but then are unable to back up their claim - like a mantra that is repeated without thinking."

— Allen O. Morris, MBA, Executive Director, Concerned Methodists

Believing that an informed, aware membership is vital to the renewal of our denomination, we present information on the expenditure of church funds. This is by no means comprehensive, but provides a means of showing what the real priorities are of our denomination's employees. The adage "follow the money" holds true in giving a reliable indicator of what one - be it individual or institution - deems important. Giving money is an affirmation of the program or body which uses it. For instance, one former executive with the General Board of Global Ministries (GBGM) attempted to tell the GBGM staff that there was resentment about perceived Board activities. One of the staff replied, "Well, if they're as upset down there as you say, they wouldn't keep sending us all this money!" [1]

I invite you to examine the "Financial Report on The United Methodist GBGM" in Annex K extracted from the more detailed "1997 Stewardship Report on the United Methodist Church" found on the Concerned Methodists website. You may also review the report by Rev. Ed Ezaki, CPA, who was on the Audit and Review Committee of the General Council on Finance and Administration (Appendix L). Both detail the accumulation of hundreds of millions of dollars in the UMC's general boards and agencies; the GBGM alone has $402,047,203.

After these two reports were published, there were the usual disclaimers that: our information was not true, our claims were exaggerated, the funds are restricted, etc., but it is interesting to note that the GBGM suddenly discovered $25 million, which it then allocated to "missions" and is using for a variety of purposes. Two questions come to mind: 1. If excess money had not been accumulated, how was it that the GBGM could suddenly make $25 million available for missions? 2. Why couldn't that money have been used to ease the burden that the apportionment poses for many of the local churches?

Since the figures from The 1997 Stewardship Report are based on 1996 statistics (the most recent available at that time), following is an analysis done by The Reverend John Warrener using 1997 data:

General Board of Global Ministries' Financial Mini-Analysis 1997:

World Service Apportionment income	$23,520,608
Stock Market and Financial Instrument Income	$60,709,471
Total Income	$192,989,212
Excess income (profit)	$52,309,176
Total Assets	$410,759,020
Direct and Indirect Missionary Support	$19,221,816

a) There are 17 years' worth of World Service Apportionment Dollars in Excess Assets!
b) The Stock Market Income of these Excess Assets earns the equivalent of almost three years of World Service Apportionment Dollars every year!
c) Excess income (profit) equals more than two years of World Service Apportionment added every year!
d) If Churches never paid another World Service Apportionment Dollar, the GBGM would continue to have income in excess of its expenses!
e) Only 10 cents of every income dollar goes to missionaries while 27 cents goes to excess assets (profit)!
— Source:Official Financial Statement of GBGM mini-analysis by John Warrener, MDiv., MBA (Master's Degree in Business Administration); taken from:http://ucmpage.org

An additional factor is that money that leaves the church in the form of the apportionment is a drain on sometimes scarce resources at the local level. Look at Village Baptist, Berean Baptist, Northwood Temple, Covenant Love, and other churches in Fayetteville, which are independent or congregational-type churches. They have the resources to buy buses, gas, etc. to go out into the local community.

When people put their money into the offering plate, giving in good faith to what they believe is the Lord's work, their donations are sometimes used inefficiently. In the,book *Rekindlng the Flame*, Professor William H. Willimon and (the late) Professor Robert L. Wilson stated that benevolent and mission causes received a smaller share of the [UM] funds:...13 percent." [down from 16 percent](2) This indicates that proportionate giving to true mission benevolence is on the decline. To apply this sense of value to our own personal lives, who among us might be satisfied with receiving 13% of the expected value from our purchases in a store? If one were to project that figure to 1996, the estimate would be 10%. In fact, the most recent calculation by Concerned Methodists shows that this figure has dropped to 8.69991%. A related question is "What happens to that other 87%?"

We are constantly told about "worshiping God with our tithes and offerings." Dr. William H. Willimon and the late Dr. Robert L. Wilson have written, "Keeping a steady flow of funds necessary to maintain the institution receives the highest priority. Despite the rhetoric, maintaining and managing the institution are what many officials feel is important." (*Rekindling the Flame,** page 63). Since less than full disclosure is provided to the people in the pews and their money is often spent in ways distasteful to them, the problem is exacerbated. In *The Faithful Christian*, Billy Graham has written, "...when legitimate Christian organizations and churches refuse to be completely open about finances they are conditioning people to accept unquestioningly the contention of the...leader that he is not accountable for his financial dealings." (3) Paying the apportionment is the first benevolent responsibility of the local church, but there is a prior obligation of the hierarchy to exercise responsible leadership so that it will merit the money paid by those same churches. Untruthfulness, withholding information, and diverting of funds constitute a breach of trust and do not reflect good leadership.

The Scripture passage from Luke 16 talks precisely to this issue of financial integrity, saying that if you are dishonest in just a little, you will be dishonest in much. The footnote to *The Wesley Study Bible* explains verses 10-12 further, "Only those who faithfully use the wealth of this world for God's kingdom will be sufficiently trustworthy to receive the true riches - new life now and a home with God for eternity." (4) Further insight is given through the parable of The Talents and accompanying footnote for Matthew 25:16, 17, 23, "The first two servants were 'good' and 'faithful'..making them responsible for their master's money for his benefit....With God, the basis of reward is not how much we have, but how faithfully we serve." (5)

One example of problematical accountability is an appeal to help retired pastors and wives in poverty made in a brochure entitled "Take Another Look." Mr. Jack Kruppenbach stated in a letter to Bishop Peter Weaver dated June 25, 1997, "The Eastern Pennsylvania Conference (EPC) and General Board of Pension and Health Benefits (GBPHB) have made frequent references, in their appeals for stewardship, to retired pastors and pastor's wives who are living in poverty." Mr. Kruppenbach has made multiple appeals to the GBPHB as to how this could have happened, with its multi-billion dollar fund. (Currently the agency's total assets have grown to $12.1 billion, as of May 31, 1999 from $11.5 billion on December 31, 1998).(6) In a subsequent letter to an EPC elder, he confirmed his phone conversation with him: "During our discussion, you advised me that the situation never did exist where actual retirees or retirees' spouses underwent those hardships (i.e., 'needing orthopedic shoes or the retired clergy living in poverty in government-subsidized housing'). You indicated that the references should never have been used...because they were only hypothetical parables of good works, when extra funding might be needed. Did I hear you correctly?" The pastor disavowed this conversation, but he is certain that is what was said. Over the space of three years, Mr. Kruppenbach has attempted repeatedly to get the names of the retired pastors and/or spouses so that he, along with others in his area, could provide more immediate help to these "faithful servants"; as of yet, Mr. Kruppenbach has received no names nor other information.

A second example (one of several of this nature) concerns Mission Church in Sierra Leone (Advance Special #00826). The Soddy-Daisy (Tennessee) United Methodist Men (UMM) and lay delegate Sherman Morton provided $7,000 to build a little mission church in Sierra Leone where there was none. Later, the UMM chapter was informed that more money was needed to build the church. Afterwards, they found out that, instead of being used to build the mission church, the money was used at the Moyiba-Kissy Brook Church, the bishop's home church. Subsequent efforts to recover the money failed, despite the services of an attorney.(7) We have heard of multiple instances of this happening across the country.

A Third example involves The first International Youth Conference for Mission (IYCM).(8) On August 10, 1999, the United Methodist Women's Division sponsored a missions training camp for teenagers from around the world. The first International Youth Conference for Mission (IYCM) convened July 3-11 at Geneva Point Center in Center Harbor, New Hampshire. The Women's Division paid for the travel of the 150 youth and 50 adults who attended. Each person's travel cost averaged about $2,000, making the total cost about $400,000.

The beginning of the week started out like any other church camp. Icebreakers were used to help everyone get to know one another, but theological persuasions eventually were revealed. The adult leaders seemed to test how far they could go with certain concepts, such as calling God Mother, or referring to people as "co-creators" with God. Sometimes students openly objected to unorthodox theological assertions or at least shared their puzzlement.

Some youth from the South Central Jurisdiction asked the camp organizers for a workshop on homosexuality. At first the leaders liked the idea, until they found out the students intended to reinforce biblical principles and official UM teachings regarding sexuality. According to some of the students, Joyce Sohl scotched their proposal, explaining that such a workshop would be too troublesome.

Some of the workshop subjects were: Mission and Justice, Racial Justice, and Environmental Justice. Some youth asked what these themes had to do with missions. Many youth were looking for practical ways to share their faith in Christ, but instead learned about the political agenda of the Women's Division. David Wildman, a seminar designer for the Women's Division, led a workshop on Violence and Justice. He claimed that Jesus was assassinated for His political beliefs.

Nicole Roskos, a student of ecological and feminist theology at Drew University, led a workshop on Environmental Justice. She performed a satire about the "Biotic Baking Brigade"(BBB). The BBB is a group of comic vigilantes who throw meringue pies in the faces of corporate "criminals" and their accomplices: Microsoft Chairman Bill Gates, Mayor Willie Brown of San Francisco, Milton Friedman, lawyer Robert Shapiro, and Sierra Club director Carl Pope. Most of the youth looked uncomfortable during the play and did not appreciate its supposed humor. A staunch advocate of civil disobedience, she told the youth that sometimes violence is necessary to combat certain injustices.... and claimed that Jesus was a radical political activist, based on His clearing the moneychangers out of the Temple. She gave advice to students on how to avoid getting arrested at protests, and how to get arrested when politically desirable.

Tamara Walker, a GBGM staff person, led the workshop on Mission and Justice. Like Roskos, she also condemned capitalism, focusing on the exploitation of foreign labor markets by large American corporations. But her solution appeared not to be based on spiritual transformation through the Gospel, but rather government regulation and control of private industry. According to a handout that Walker distributed, our "mission is to challenge the false gods of our times": ego-centrism, materialism, militarism, economic exploitation, exploitation of the earth, race, class and gender privilege, etc.

Throughout the conference the youth questioned statements from workshop leaders. A young woman stood up and read the first stated goal of the GBGM: to witness to the Gospel for initial decision to follow Jesus Christ. Upon finishing she asked, "If this is a missions conference, and this is your number one goal, then why hasn't it even been mentioned?" The adult leaders seemed unable to respond.

Stewardship is important to God. How about to us?

Notes:
1. *The Faith that Compels Us* by Dr. H. T. Maclin, The Mission Society for United Methodists, 6234 Crooked Creek Rd., Norcross, GA 30092; p. 32.
2. *Rekindling the Flame*, p. 19.
3. *The Faithful Christian* by Billy Graham, McCracken Press, New York; 1994, p. 113.
4. *The Wesley Study Bible*, pub. by Thomas Nelson, Nashville, Tennessee, 1990, p. 1552.
5. Ibid, p. 1461.
6. United Methodist News Service (UMNS) #384; July 22, 1999; Nashville, Tenn.; 10-31-71B{384}.
7. Correspondence from the former pastor of the Soddy-Daisy United Methodist Church, their attorney involved in the situation, and the attorney for the General Board of Global Ministries.
8. Mark Tooley and Holland Webb; Institute on Religion and Democracy; http://ucmpage.org/umaction/mtooley42.htm; Aug 12 13:06:17 1999.

4

Agents of Change - Issues

"It is important to recognize the linkages among the component parts of the sexual revolution. Permissive abortion, widespread adultery, easy divorce, radical feminism, and the gay and lesbian movement have not by accident appeared at the same historical moment. They have in common a declared desire for liberation from constraint - especially constraints associated with an allegedly oppressive culture and religious tradition."

- The Ramsey Colloquium+ (1)

If we are to examine "flag" issues in our denomination today, they range from secular sociopolitical advocacy and "Re-Imagining" Theologies to moral areas such as homosexuality and abortion.

Sociopolitical Causes*

During the 1972 - 1980 time period, a program was initiated that resulted in a document called "The Bishops' Call for Peace and the Self-Development of Peoples," which was presented in 1972 by Bishop A. James Armstrong. This document called for developing programs based on global internationalism and for greater utilization of the United Nations as opposed to national self-determination. The report to the 1976 General Conference clarified the Bishops' Call: "To be frank about it, the church has to take responsibility for the political education of its constituency...." (2) This reflects the philosophy espoused by bishops C. P. Minnick, Jr., Ernest T. Dixon, Jr., and Kenneth W. Hicks. They stated, "As Christian peacemakers we must use our skills of international diplomacy..."(3) As one who has studied, worked, and lived in the international environment for forty-three years, I cannot help but ask, "What skills?" This same perspective was observed by Dr. John Silber, then president of Boston University, the largest UM-related university: "The bishops have not demonstrated either the historical and contemporary knowledge or the diplomatic and military experience necessary to speak with authority on the Nicaraguan question or the intricate question of disarmament."(4) The 1989 study by Concerned Methodists of the bishops' pronouncements on Nicaragua (Appendix C) offers additional background. Their conclusions were at variance with reality and what subsequently happened in the Sandinistas being ousted by the nationalist Violeta Chamorro. Two similar views are those of Phil Shriver ("The Methodist Syndrome" at Appendix B) and Rev. Max Borah ("Missionary Orientation" at Appendix I). One can read other examples in the books *Biases and Blind Spots* and *The Betrayal of the Church*, which can be found on the Concerned Methodists' website.

A national publication reviewed this same perspective in the National Council of Churches (NCC): "A number of NCC (i.e., National Council of Churches) executives feel a just society is impossible under capitalism. In 1975, an Ecumenical Consultation on Domestic Hunger sponsored by the NCC passed a statement that said there was a basic contradiction between capitalism 'and biblical justice, mercy, stewardship, service, community and self-giving love.' Similar antagonistic views toward the American economic system are evident in the publications of the NCC's Friendship Press and in NCC-sponsored films."(5)

Finally, we question personnel using church resources to lobby for political positions that are contrary to those of a significant number of members of the United Methodist Church while appearing to speak for them.

"Re-Imagining" and "goddess" Theologies*

A nascent radical feminist theology has sought to replace Jesus Christ as the object of worship with female deities. The Re-Imagining Conference (see Appendix D) occurred over six years ago but continues to have repercussions to this day. After it happened, objections to what transpired at this event were met with untruths or spins. Sadly, George Jones, who was pastor of my own Camp Ground UMC at the time, used some of them at a March 6, 1994 Council on Ministries meeting.

Spin: "This was a one time event. It's a dead issue."
Truth: The Sophia/goddess timeline at Appendix D belies this argument.

Spin: "Goddess worship did not actually occur."
Truth: Terminology and the liturgy used testify that in fact this did happen: "Our maker, Sophia, we are women in your image...," "Sophia, we celebrate your life-giving energy which pulses through our veins..." (from the "Re-Imagining handbook)

Spin: "It's not a problem; only 391 United Methodist women attended."
Truth: Whether or not it is perceived as a "problem" depends on the reality of the person and work of Jesus Christ, Who affirms the atonement, salvation, and spiritual lostness.

Spin: "Methodists did not support this conference."
Truth: In addition to the planning, $37,581 was paid for 36 directors, 9 staff and 11 UMW conference VPs to attend.

Spin: "How do you know this this was a problem? You weren't there."
Truth: Neither were we in the Nazi holocaust, World War II, and the Korean War, but we're pretty sure of what happened during each of those events.

Homosexuality*

"Have you ever watched a sand castle begin its crumble as the tide advances? It's a study in erosion. First, the foundation is undermined. Then the walls begin to sag. Finally the entire structure comes crashing down. Erosion is like that...even in the Christian life. A habit that you once considered unthinkable is grudgingly tolerated. And what you tolerate is all too soon condoned...then endorsed...then openly promoted as acceptable in God's eyes."(6)

In order to promote homosexuality, one must discount the biblical view that God's standard for us in terms of sexuality is between husband and wife within the context of marriage. A review of past decisions and actions leading up to the present found in "Historical Homosexual Highlights" at Appendix E would show that our denomination is increasingly supportive of this lifestyle. The note on Bishop C. P. Minnick's letterhead urging UM pastors in the North Carolina Conference to attend a two day seminar sponsored by a homosexual advocacy group is at Appendix F. The news release of the "Denver 15" bishops themselves is found at Appendix G. Information on this lifestyle has been provided in "A Snapshot of the Gay Lifestyle" at Appendix H.

Abortion*

My people are destroyed for lack of knowledge. — Hosea 4:6

Since our denomination is supportive of "choice" in the area of abortion, we simply ask that you look at two of the most compelling verses found in the Bible regarding life issues found in Psalm 139:13-16; and Jeremiah 1:5; and read the experiences of a lady, Ms. Judy Mamou, who underwent this procedure:

"It's been a long time since the lights went out and the doctors went home. But the memory of the few hours I spent in an abortion clinic will be with me to my grave.

I remember the fear I felt lying in the cold white room surrounded by men and women in clean white uniforms. I remember the cold metal stirrups I was told to put my feet in and the cold metal instrument that was inserted into my body to open me up. Most of all I remember the suction machine sucking the life of the baby from within me. The sound of the baby being vacuumed out never goes away.

The doctor may act very kindly and assure you that it will all be over in a few minutes. But how can it be, when you later discover or realize that they lied when they told you it wasn't a person inside you?

Where is the doctor now as I lie here in the still of the night hearing the noise of the vacuum, feeling the cold metal and seeing in my mind's eye the bits and pieces of my baby being sucked through the tube of the suction machine? Where was the doctor all those years that I woke up screaming, hearing babies crying in the night?

The sound of the suction machine haunts me to this day. I cannot vacuum a floor without thinking of my abortion.

I never look at a child and not wonder: was mine a boy or a girl; blond or brunette; my baby would be that age if only....

I have been raped, beaten, a victim of incest and many other things in life but the thing that haunts me most is I let people kill a child of mine. I didn't know at the time that it was a life. I was told it was a blob, matter, nothing, like a tumor to be removed. One day it hits you: it was not a blob or a mass of tissue. It was a BABY!

I can never undo what I allowed to happen but with the forgiveness I have from Jesus I can live with it and do my part to help others not to make the same mistake I did."(7)

Each of these areas represent troubling issue, but are in reality just the symptoms of deeper, more fundamental problems in our church.

+ The Ramsey Colloquium is sponsored by the Institute on Religion and Public Life. The Colloquium is a group of Jewish and Christian theologians, ethicists, philosophers, and scholars who meet periodically to consider questions on morality, religion, and public life. It is named after Paul Ramsey (1913 - 1988), the distinguished Methodist ethicist.

Notes:
1. The Ramsey Colloquium,+ as quoted in *First Things*, editor: Father Richard John Neuhaus; March, 1994, p. 17.

2. *Biases and Blind Spots*, by the late Dr. Robert L. Wilson, Bristol House Ltd., P.O. Box 4020, Anderson, IN 46013; 1991, pp. 63 - 64.

3. From a brochure entitled "Report of the Council of Bishops on the Mission of Peace to Nicaragua," dated May 1, 1985, p. 16.

4. "University president indicts UM theology, politics," *The United Methodist Reporter*, June 10, 1988; p. 3.

5. "Do You Know Where Your Church Offerings Go?" by Rael Jean Isaacs; *Readers Digest*, January 1983.

6. *The Daily Walk*, published by The Navigators, P. O. Box 6000, Colorado Springs, Colorado 80934; August 1, 1993.

7. "The Fear I Felt" by Judy Mamou, by Life Cycle Books, P. O. Box 420, Lewiston, NY 19092-0420. Permission to reprint granted.

* A more detailed description of UM involvement in this area can be found on the Concerned Methodists website.

5

Institutional Dynamics

"In the church's bureaucracy, the emphasis on survival takes the form of extreme defensiveness of the status quo. Any questioning of organizational procedures or programs evokes a defensive and negative response. Critics will be labeled as disloyal trouble makers. When leaders are chosen, creativity, courage, and vision will be valued less than loyalty to the status quo. The impression is conveyed that the church is an extremely fragile institution that will suffer irreparable damage if its most loyal supporters raise...questions."(1)

The fact that hundreds of people are employed in a plethora of activities and spending hundreds of millions of dollars each year is a distant reality to most of the people in the pews of the local churches, whose offerings support this activity. As Phil Shriver has stated in "The Methodist Syndrome" (Appendix B) it is difficult to relate to them. This experience is reinforced by those of of Rev. Max Borah (Appendix I) and Dr. Karl Stegall (Appendix J).

Institutional Models
The function of our denomination has been compared to that of a military hierarchy by some in the clergy ranks themselves: bishops are the generals; the district superintendents are the colonels; the local church pastors are the captains; and the laity are the privates. This parallels the institutional view that the pastor is the "executive agent" of the general church. There are two problems associated with this. One is that this makes the local church dysfunctional, since the pastor who thinks of himself as the captain is supposed to command the laity who are the privates, but who also pay his salary. The church has also been compared to the government with respect to paying the apportionment ("taxes"), with the explanation that we are not always happy with how our leaders spend our tax money, but we pay taxes anyway. But neither of

these apply. If we were to use any secular model, then perhaps the commercial, free marketplace might come closer to reality, since it illustrates the freedom that God gives us to grow, make choices, and to function as rational human beings. But, the church should be the church - and not resemble any secular model.

Institutionalism

The functioning of the institutional church seems to follow the pattern of requirements being passed "down" to the local church from the bishop, district superintendent, and the general boards and agencies. Rather than spiritual transformation that results in changed lives, we have evolved into a "works righteousness" denomination that is increasingly focused on meeting the socio/physical needs of others while not speaking to their deeper spiritual yearnings and at the same time experiencing an ever greater degree of standardization and control. Dr. William H. Willimon and the late Dr. Robert L. Wilson wrote, "Our system is being misused for the benefit of certain groups.(2) A key issue facing the United Methodist Church today is that of "institutionalism." The self-perpetuation of the institution appears to be a top priority.

Leadership

"If my company had lost 13 percent of its business in the last twenty years, I would be out of a job," one corporate vice president told us. - Dr. William H. Willimon and the late Dr. Robert L. Wilson (3)

One of the qualities necessary for good leadership is to face, admit, and correct problems. A chief responsibility for the decline in the United Methodist Church lies squarely at the feet of the bishops. It is this body which is invested with leading the church. In their book, Dr. Willimon and the late Dr. Wilson stated that a problem we have in the denomination is that we have managers, not leaders. The problems is that managers "accept the validity of the institutional status quo and give their attention to its maintenance."(4) To cite some specific examples of leadership problems we have:

a. Our denomination has an unbroken 29-year history of decline in membership (see Appendix A), but the bishops have yet to analyze why it has occurred.

b. The public position taken by two separate delegations of bishops to Nicaragua in the 1980s exhibited the fact that they did not have a sound base of knowledge of the situation there (see Appendix C).

c. Not one active bishop openly condemned the 1993 "Re-Imagining Conference" for the rank heresy and apostasy that it was (see the Re-Imagining Time Line at Appendix D). If Jesus is central to our faith (and He should be) and if a bishop truly held him up as Lord and Savior, he would not hesitate to have taken strong action against it.

d. In April 1996 the "Denver 15" United Methodist bishops issued a press release calling for the ordination of homosexuals in opposition to sound medical evidence against that lifestyle, the UMC's officially stated position, a majority of UMs, the Book of Discipline, and the Bible. If a military general had publicly condemned his army's operations, he would have been fired. If a CEO had publicly criticized his company's product, he too would have been fired. Principles of sound leadership dictate that supervisory personnel do not publicly criticize organizational policies or products; to do so is seen as exhibiting weak leadership. In the secular arena, the "Denver 15" bishops would have been fired or received other disciplinary action.

e. Prior to the 1996 General Conference in Denver, Colorado, Mel Brown had written Bishop Mary Ann Swenson (one of the "Denver 15") about problems in the church; he never received a reply. Subsequently, he took out ads in two area newspapers airing those same problems to an estimated half million people. After the Conference was over, she and her cabinet traveled to Johnstown, Colorado, to meet with him. After they had discussed the issues, she then asked him, "Well, Mr. Brown. Do you still think I should resign?" He leaned over, looked her in the eyes, and responded, "You bet I do." If Bishop Swenson had taken the time to respond to legitimate concerns, which is a function of responsible leadership, she might not have exacerbated her problems.

f. The bishops appear to be incapable of enforcing the Book of Discipline in the performance of "same-sex" ceremonies (See Appendix E), yet have shown the capacity to take swift, decisive action when necessary: Bishop Lindsey Davis in dismissing Dr. Charles Sineath, and Bishop Ann Sherer in doing the same with Dr. Ron Cansler, pastor of FUMC in Joplin, Missouri. Is their inability to resolve the "same-sex problems" in reality covert acceptance of this advocacy? It would appear so.

Institutional Personalities

We have found different personages and behaviors that are, to a great extent, predictable:

The Company Man/Woman (CM/W). As related to us by Dr. Michael Tyler (Tennessee AC), their pastor had said,"I am a company man. I have always been a company man. And I will always be a company man." CM/Ws are found throughout the denomination, attempt to exercise a spirit of control, and are obedient to their "top down" chain of command regardless of the instructions. Two of the most important functions of CM/Ws in the local church seem to be to get the apportionment paid and to "keep the people under control." This was reinforced by Dr. Willimon and the late Dr. Wilson when they wrote, "...there is a tendency for the clergy to feel that their future lies and that their ministry will be evaluated, not by their service to the local congregation, but by their loyalty to and compatibility with the annual conference." (5) It may be that he exhibits a love for the people in his charge, but one of the most important things that laypeople of a church (or the members of a conference) need to ascertain is what their pastor (or bishop) does with the truth. Does he adhere to it, or does he shade, distort, suppress, or withhold it? This is important and constitutes an integrity issue. The Bible speaks forcefully on this, "Therefore each of you must put off falsehood and speak truthfully to his neighbor" (Ephesians 4:25).

Other personalities are: **The Pastor with Integrity (PWI):** these are men and women who will not compromise their integrity regardless of the cost and are willing to give complete factual information to the people in their pastoral care, acting with their best interests in mind. **The Consenting Follower (CF)** is the layperson who does what he is told regardless of the rationale, or lack thereof. Sometimes, it is to defend a clergy or program, and to become properly "outraged" if either is questioned. **The Independently Thinking Person [Lay or Clergy] (ITP)** is the individual who will analyze and question what he is told, and compare pastoral pronouncements with biblical teachings.

While the bishops have a leadership responsibility in the decline of the UMC, the Consenting Followers have the fundamental responsibility since they unquestioningly accept whatever they are told. Dr. H. T. Maclin put it this way when he talked about "the almost blind trust and loyalty many United Methodist people have in our connectional system. The thought that anything could possibly be wrong in the church is simply too painful for many Methodists to bear.... Too many prefer to turn a deaf ear and hope the system will somehow cleanse itself. Unfortunately,...as Edmund Burke said, 'All that is necessary for evil to triumph is for good men to do nothing.'"(6)

Dynamics

Every half-truth is a full lie. - Pastor Richard Wurmbrand (7)

Truth. After a speech by Lindsey Davis, bishop of the Atlanta Area, in Tulsa, Oklahoma, I approached him to take issue with one of the things he had said, that a cause for problems in our denomination was the leadership at the local church level. I told him, "Bishop Davis. There are three main problems in the United Methodist Church today: the lack of truthfulness throughout the denomination, the irresponsible use of money, and a lack of responsible Christian leadership in the Council of Bishops." I then handed him a copy of "The 1997 Stewardship Report on the United Methodist Church" and recommended that he read it.

Many in the UMC have a problem with the truth. In our pursuit of various issues in the political, ethical, and spiritual realm, simply put, "truth" is often missing, especially when people question areas such as how denominational money is spent, ecclesial actions, priorities espoused, and clergy integrity. When we do bring out the truth, as painful as it is, we encounter unfounded denials and meet reactions that we are "divisive" and "trying to harm the church" in our efforts. Identifying unpleasant truths about an organization is the first step in addressing its problems; it is "divisive" only to those who are threatened by it.

In a letter sent to Bishop Kenneth L. Carder dated October 4, 1996 (by certified mail), I had written: "Dear Bishop Carder: I have received a copy of your letter to Dr. Michael L. Tyler (Finance Committee Chair and Lay leader of FUMC - Mt. Pleasant) dated September 24, 1996... I find it curious that you characterize our data as being 'false,' 'misleading,' 'distortions,' and 'misinformation.' Yet it is my understanding that you have requested information from Dr. Randy Nugent to prepare for your meeting with members of the Finance Committee of FUMC of Mt. Pleasant on October 21st. How can you attack our data as being 'false' and with the other adjectives you have if you do not feel you have adequate information in your possession at this time. ....I invite you to publicly debate these issues with me at a time and place of mutual convenience...." In his letter dated October 8, 1996, he declined to meet me in public debate. (Since we research and are comfortable with the accuracy of our data before it is published, we invariably challenge our accusers to a public debate, because then people will see what the truth really is.) We have had similar encounters with other UM clergy, among whom are Helen Crotwell (past superintendent of the Fayetteville District), Randy Mickler (preacher at Mt. Bethel UMC in Acworth, Georgia), and George Jones (recent preacher at my own church), to name a few.

Pedestalization of the Minister. As Chuck Swindoll has written, "I believe it is the minister whom the people tend most to pedestalize. It is certainly an unscriptural practice. The Berean believers are commended for listening to Paul, then '...examining the

Scriptures daily, to see whether these things were so' (Acts 17:11)."(8) Dr. Willimon and the late Dr. Wilson called this the "halo effect" in their book *Rekindling the Flame*. (9)

Incrementalism. A well thought-out plan of incrementalism appears to be used. "Incrementalism" consists of small, barely noticeable changes deliberately made over a period of time, which have had a cumulative effect in changing the essence of our denomination. This process is best illustrated by an incident observed by Chuck Swindoll when he was in high school. He writes, "I watched the slow death of a frog in an unforgettable experiment [from his high school chemistry class]. My teacher placed the hapless creature in an oversized beaker of cool water. Beneath the beaker he moved a Bunsen burner with a very low flame so that the water heated very slowly - something like .017 of a degree Fahrenheit per second. In fact, the temperature rose so gradually that the frog was never aware of the change. Two and a half hours later the frog was dead...boiled to death. The change occurred so slowly that the frog neither tried to jump out nor released a complaining kick."(10) This can have the effect of moving a majority of the membership in our UMC away from the Orthodox Christian faith to another by a series of small, barely noticeable changes. One overall effect of incrementalism is that through the continuous influx of new people with "Ten Dollar Religion" and the exodus of older and/or more spiritually mature members through departure and death, the spiritual character of the United Methodist Church is being changed.

A Spirit of control. Pastor Sineath told Good News magazine: "We've been part of a system for 38 years that prides itself on its tolerance and tolerates many things we believe God has declared unacceptable. Yet that same system has demonstrated its absolute intolerance of any dissent that has a dollar sign attached to it."(11) Some who occupy positions in the institution of the UMC have spans of control, want to extend their influence, are reluctant to justify what they do to anyone, and strive to maintain that control.

Information Control. This appears to be common practice in the Church, by both CM/Ws and evangelical pastors as well. There seems to be an active effort to withhold information from the people in the pews. In a letter, Helen Crotwell, past superintendent of the Fayetteville District, used an expression common to this spirit of control to not talk to us because it is not useful; indeed, it is not useful to the institutional church because the more these issues are discussed, the more people will be aware of the deep-seated problems we have. Mrs. Barbara Wendland has hypothesized on this spirit of control in her publication *Connections* when she had attempted to get a copy of the list of the names and addresses of the delegates to her annual conference. She also talks about the experiences of Ms. Garlinda Burton (with the *UM Reporter*) when she reported on the revision of The UM Hymnal and a flurry of letters resulted over the news that "Onward Christian Soldiers" would not be included in the new one. Burton said that "leaders were upset that the media had 'stirred up a fuss' and 'upset the people in the pew.'" "Pressure continues from some agency heads and episcopal leaders," she found, "to keep controversy and 'negative' information out of the hands of the church and public media - and, therefore, away from the rank and file." Mrs. Wendland also commented that "The church continues to lose credibility with each attempt to control information." They see leaders merely trying to protect each other, unwilling to confront the tough issues. Efforts to restrict information, Burton finds, have a "devastating effect on the credibility of the church bureaucracy among both grass-roots members and the public." Mrs. Wendland made the point that: "The legitimate way of combating views that one opposes is to provide information and views that are convincing, not by trying to stifle the views one disagrees with. When UMC officials only allow the expression of opinions and information that support official policies and methods, they destroy the effect [of] our representative system of church government. Annual Conference members need to hear members' views and to take them into account in making the church's decisions."(12)

Working behind the scenes. One example of how Julia McLean Williams was systematically excluded from her positions was when she started to question the General Board of Global Ministries, and later worked for the Mission Society for United Methodists ("So Great a Cloud," which is a case study in Appendix M). One of the reasons that CMWs work behind the scenes is because they know that if these issues were discussed publicly, people would learn the truth.

Gossip. One very effective tool is that of gossip. For the individual who does indulge in this practice, it is an indication of weak character. It's easy to talk about someone when he is not around; it takes more courage to face him and discuss the problem with him in person. After all, the gossip may be, and probably is, wrong. Gossip is like a contagious disease that poisons the mind: it can spread and do a lot of harm. Chuck Swindoll had this to say about it in a game he called "Let's Label": "...it is important that we guard against using a wrong label, thus damaging that individual's true image or position in others' eyes. That is the main danger in playing "Let's Label". It often means you set yourself up as judge and jury, declaring information that is exaggerated or thirdhand or just plain untrue. When that happens, we have stopped playing a game and started to slander." He goes on to say, "...basing one's opinion on the absolute truth is a sign of maturity, a mark of excellence in life....(Proverbs 12:17-23)"(13) In a spiritual vein, this violates the instructions Jesus gave us in Matthew 18:15 and those from Paul in Galatians 6:1.

Strategy

Following are some of the methods that we believe are used in the promotion of the institutional agenda and that exhibit the characteristics of a concerted, intentional strategy:

Stacking the boards. A Company Man will try to stack the boards to get the "right people" (i.e., "Consenting Follower") into key positions, those whom he can control: Administrative Board,

Council on Finance, Council on Ministries, Pastor/Staff Parish Relations, lay delegate to annual conference, etc.

Focusing on the local church. It should be noted that, in reality, the local church is what should be the primary focus of ministry throughout the UMC. As has already been stated, there are a lot of good things happening at this level (observed in "The Methodist Syndrome"). But we still must have an interest in what is occurring at the general church level, because what happens there will ultimately affect every local church in our denomination. This tactic is what enabled the injustices to be perpetrated against other churches, such as St. Francis UMC (Appendix Q) and Kingsburg UMC (Appendix R) in the California-Nevada Conference. We need to remember that we are "all members of one body; what happens to one affects the whole body."

Encouraged passivity. This is a corollary of "Focusing on the local church." Many of the laity who populate the pews of many churches today are mentally passive. They have succumbed to the climate of control, and abrogated their responsibility to provide informed lay leadership and effective feedback.

Targeting. In 1984, Charles Keysor asked the question, "Just what is United Methodism like?...Many mainline Methodists boast that the church's greatest asset is pluralism. Yet, oddly, evangelicals are consistently excluded from the highest elective and major policy-making positions."(14) There seems to be an institutional policy of systematically excluding from positions of leadership and influence in the church those who are independent thinkers. Dr. Julia Williams experienced this after she started to question the unresponsiveness of one of our church's boards (Appendix M).

The pattern seems to be that a CM/W might be sent to a church with the objective of neutralizing ITPs. The profile of the new Company Man will be that of "a really nice guy" with "just the sweetest wife in the world" that a person would ever want to meet. He will be affable, deliver great "feel good" sermons, and involve the people in "busy work" to get their minds off the problems facing the denomination. He will work his Consenting Followers into key positions in church leadership and exclude the leading ITPs. He will put monitors in classes ITPs attend to report back what is said and any influence he may have; the monitor may attempt to neutralize any influence he may have on other class members. He may orchestrate a variety of tactics to encourage ITPs to leave the church and even the denomination. In addition, if the members of a congregation receive information from an independent source, they will be encouraged to discontinue receipt of these publications. Dr. Williams appears to have been targeted in her narrative, as have Marty Rasmussen, Jimmy Cash, and I, because of our association with renewal organizations. Another whom appears to have been targeted is Mel Brown in Johnstown, Colorado, who is associated with Concerned Methodists of the Rocky Mountains.

Orchestrated Silence. When people receive information on some of the unpleasant problems in the church, they are told, "It's not profitable to discuss this with these people. Just ignore it." This effectively neutralizes any effort to address some of the issues, and is a common tactic across the UMC. We have recently received complaints of this happening in some of the Texas conferences. Unfortunately, there are those in my own church who have succumbed to this. I sent Jay Spillane a letter* dated December 6, 1996 requesting data on defamatory information communicated by George Jones (later shown to be false); Jay returned the letter unopened and refused to answer my questions. It is difficult to understand how a guy like Jay, a retired Army colonel and the father of two kids (a boy and a girl) for whom I'd been a youth counselor, would have acted in such a manner. In addition, despite the fact that I had been a youth counselor for the children of Steve Thomas and Barbara Poole (his son and daughter, and her two sons), when I was seeking information of a similar nature circulated by George Jones, they refused to speak with me or even to discuss it. (See "Camp Ground UMC" at Appendix T for additional information. The complete letter to Jay Spillane is in the CGUMC Case Study on the Concerned Methodists' internet website.)

One well-intentioned guy who had previously refused to discuss the church's problems, engaged me in conversation one day. We had a good discussion, with his asking me about my varied assignments, where I had been, what I had done, and accomplishments. After he had exhausted his questions, I then responded, "Look, I have answered all of your questions. Now, answer mine. I have been in the Army, just like you. I have been stationed at Ft. Bragg, as you are. I was once a major, just as you are now. When I had attempted to talk with you previously about the problems in the church, you refused. Why is that?"

He: "Because I don't agree with what you say! I don't agree with what you stand for."

I: "With what do you not agree?"

He: "All of it!"

I: "Name one."

There was silence. Complete silence. In other words, he had been manipulated into automatically rejecting the information because it was from us, yet without knowing what it was we were saying - or why.

It is as if people have been brainwashed.

Notes:
1. Rekindling the Flame,* page 17.
2. Ibid., p. 121.
3. Ibid., p. 68.
4. Ibid., pp. 58, 59.
5. Ibid., p. 108.
6. Faith, p. 32.
7. The Absolute Duty of Truthfulness" in Alone with God, by Pastor Richard Wurmbrand, Living Sacrifice Book Company, Bartlesville, OK; 1988, p. 36.
8. "Fallibility" from Come Before Winter, p. 58.
9. Rekindling the Flame, p. 67.
10. Growing Strong in the Seasons of Life, by Chuck Swindoll, Multnomah Press, Portland, Oregon, 1977; p. 93.

11. Article in World, as quoted in an e-mail received from Janz I. Mynderup; <vision@newpathways.com>; Subject: Split...Today?? Date: Sat, 26 Jun 1999 23:14:03.
12. Connections by Barbara Wendland, 505 Cherokee Drive, Temple, TX 76504, May 1999. Permission to reprint granted.
13. "Labels" from Come Before Winter; pp. 112 - 113.
14. As quoted from Christianity Today, November 9, 1984 in "Methodism 1784 - 1984." By Charles Yoh, Van Wert, Ohio; 1986, p. 16.

* Available on the Concerned Methodists website.

6

The Institutional
and the Local Church

It is understood that in the workings of organizational entities, there will be friction and misunderstandings. But we have encountered multiple instances where this seemed excessive, as if the local churches were being abused. Several case studies which exemplify a variety of problems between various people in the institutional church and local churches are: Ocracoke UMC on Ocracoke Island in North Carolina (Appendix N); First UMC of Omaha, Nebraska (Appendix O); Salem UMC of Lodi, California (Appendix P); St. Francis UMC in San Francisco, California (Appendix Q); First UMC of Kingsburg, California (Appendix R); First UMC of Marietta, Georgia (Appendix S); and Camp Ground UMC of Fayetteville, North Carolina (Appendix T). For instance, at Salem UMC of Lodi, California, 27 people were notified that they had been removed from the rolls of the UMC. Following are three others with more summarized information:

High Point District (Western North Carolina Conference). According to information given to us, Richard Crowder, superintendent of the High Point district, closed Randolph Hills UMC, a viable, working church, and turned it into his own district office.

Seibert UMC, Seibert, Colorado (Rocky Mountain Conference). As the situation was reported to us, the D.S. went into the local bank and asked to look at the account for the Seibert UMC. The clerk informed the president, who attended that church. The D.S. was told, that there was no way that he would be permitted to look at the account. The people, alerted to this action, opened other bank accounts with no direct connection to their church and operated from them. They then safeguard their assets, accumulated sufficient funds, purchased their church from the conference, and then formed an independent church.

Hillrose UMC, Hillrose, Colorado (Rocky Mountain Conference). As the situation was reported to us by Mr. Gene Peterson and Mrs. Jo Ann Windolf who belong to the church, the members of their congregation had accumulated $16,000 to pay for repairs on the building to the roof and the windows, and to paint the church. According to Mr. Peterson, the people are farmers and that money "came pretty hard" as he put it. A pastor that they had (and who did not have legal access to the church's bank account) took the money and cleaned out the safe deposit box; later the conference sold the parsonage. Subsequently, the district superintendent locked the doors of the church and left town. Since the people had keys to the building, they would open it on Sundays and have their own laity-led church services. When officials from the conference found out about this, they changed the locks on the building. Through subsequent negotiations, the people bought the church for $8,000 (which they termed a "ransom") with a note signed by Mr. Peterson. Mrs. Windolf, who is a farmer's wife herself, said, "People just don't know to what lengths they [i.e., the conference] will go to get their hands on property that isn't theirs." The people had bought the land and the building, paid for its upkeep, and cared for it over the years. Both indicated that the people of the church are pretty bitter over what happened. As a result of these and other actions in the conference, they projected that other United Methodist churches in the area would soon close due to decreased attendance: Snider (3-4 people), Antelope Springs (3-4 people), and Willard.

In personal correspondence, how many times do we see letters begin or conclude with "Grace and peace," yet the words and actions that follow reflect the opposite? This dissonance seems to apply to "connetionalism."

7

Operative Theology

On Tuesday, August 19, 1997, The Reverend Pritchard Adams, III boarded the USAir flight bound from Charlotte, North Carolina to Sarasota, Florida. From there he would catch one of the flights headed to Haiti where he had served as a missionary for over fourteen years. He introduced himself to the lady in the seat next to him, who confided how depressed she was that her first husband had died and a second marriage had ended in divorce, and about her life in general. Rev. Adams talked with her and found out that she had been a (United) Methodist for her entire life of 80+ years. Further discussion revealed that she was not a Christian. Starting with the reason for Christ's coming to earth and ending with the resurrection, he invited her to accept Jesus as her personal Savior; she did. When the plane landed in Sarasota, she met her family in a much happier spirit and was praising the Lord. Rev. Adams, who is not a United Methodist, wondered how this elderly lady, a great-grandmother, could have been in church for her entire life and not known how to become a Christian.

- Personal interview with The Reverend Pritchard Adams, III.

This exemplifies one of the fundamental problems in the United Methodist Church - the spiritual poverty of many members in our denomination - having a form of religion but not the substance. We believe this is for two primary reasons:

1. Many if not most UMs have not had their lives changed by having truly accepted Jesus Christ as Lord and savior. This is what Dr. E. Stanley Jones lamented over forty years ago. What is missed is the life-changing nature of Jesus Christ. This has resulted from the erosion of the vibrant faith that was experienced by the early founders of Methodism and by some in our denomination today. We cannot underestimate the damage this poses, not only to the debilitation of the UMC, but in individual lives as well. We need to

consider the eternal dimensions of our spirituality; what happens to a person when he leaves this life? Heaven is a possibility; are they on the right path to get there? We must also consider hell; as unpleasant as it is for us to think about it, that, too, is real, and the possibility is great that a significant number of our members will go there. How does that happen? Most often, it is through the gradual erosion of our faith, resulting in ""Ten Dollar Religion" that gives the illusion of spirituality but is only an imitation. C.S. Lewis put it this way, "The safest road to hell is the gradual one - the gentle slope, soft underfoot, without sudden turnings, without milestones, without signposts. The long, dull, monotonous years of middle-aged prosperity or adversity are excellent campaigning weather for the devil."(1)

2. The second is the loss of the authority of the Bible as God's Word. If we do not have a source of authority, we are like a ship on the high seas without a compass: on a course but not knowing where we are headed. We have nothing on which to build a theological foundation.

These are tied to a corollary view that the process of institutionalism has led us to "another agenda" having supplanted Jesus Christ as the de facto center of the United Methodist Church.

Notes:
1. As quoted by Chuck Swindoll in *Seasons of Life*, p. 353.

8

Prognosis for the Future

From an analysis of the "fruits" of past activities and emphases, we believe that these are the directions in which we are headed:

* It appears that our church leadership is moving the UMC down a road away from the orthodox Christian faith.

* It appears that our church leadership use a consensus of the Council of Bishops as their operative authority, rather than the Bible or the *Book of Discipline*.

* The increased numbers of news releases about benevolent activities and the "bishops initiatives" serve to camouflage the deeper problems that are potentially undermining the UMC.

* Increased political activism under the banner of "shalom" will be used to support themes such as global disarmament, internationalism, and a world without borders.(1)

* The merging with other denominations will proceed as the uniqueness of salvation through Jesus Christ is minimized, reaching accords with other faiths such as Islam and Buddhism.

* It is believed that the bishops want to "dialogue" about the homosexual issue to wear down opposition to its practice so that it will ultimately be normalized.

* As the children who are raised in the church progress through the various youth programs, they will be subjected to more information that teach moral relativism. Consequently, a larger percentage will be led into sexually promiscuous lifestyles. This, in turn, will lead to greater instances of unwanted pregnancies, single motherhood, abortions, and ill-advised marriages. As they are immersed

in a climate that is increasingly supportive of homosexual practice, more will start to view that lifestyle with ever greater degrees of sympathy and will become involved in it.

* The greatest tragedy is that countless thousands if not millions of people will never know what it means to have a truly Spirit-filled relationship with, nor salvation through, Jesus Christ.

* Ever increasing degrees of control will be exercised over local churches, clergy, and laypeople.

* It is anticipated that evangelicals and independent thinkers will ultimately be forced out of the church, as has happened in some cases in California. As more independent thinkers leave and greater "top-down" control is exercised over the United Methodist Church, it will slip into bondage.

Note:
1. "UMs should be evangelists for God's shalom" by Edward C. Perry; United Methodist Review, Dallas, Texas; May 28, 1999, p. 5.

9

Revival - What is Needed?

A Million Dollar Relationship with Jesus Christ!

Many people remember a television show in the 1950s called "The Millionaire". If you will recall the sequence, in the first half of the program, a person would be going through different problems in life and experiencing a lot of emotional turmoil. Then there would be a knock on the door; when it was opened, a Mr. Anthony would introduce himself and the purpose for his visit. He was employed by an eccentric multi-billionare who would give selected people a gift of one million dollars - tax free. The two conditions stipulated were that the recipient could not tell anyone else the source of the money, nor how much. Usually, Mr. Anthony would have to spend several minutes convincing the recipient that the offer was genuine. In the second half of the show, the person would usually have a changed life, having achieved a complete turnaround in his fortunes - and his attitude.

Earlier, we had referred to "Ten Dollar Religion" as being a cause of decline in our denomination. The "Million Dollar" relationship with Jesus Christ is more than just a comparison of the dollar amounts; it represents the transforming effect He has on our lives. The only difference between this and the television show above (aside from TV's fictional nature) is that we can and should tell others about it. It is just like a stack of checks, each for one million dollars, made out to every member of the UMC. Jesus explains it best in John 10:10, "I have come that they may have life and have it to the full."

But there is a second aspect to accepting Jesus as Lord and Savior: the assurance of where we will be after we die. We need to look at things from God's perspective and recognize that there are truths, whether we believe them or not. Heaven is real. Hell is real. Each person who calls himself a United Methodist will spend eternity in one place or the other. Where will you be? Where will your children be?

This means that each of us needs to:

1. Recognize that all of us are sinners: bishops, clergy, and laity (Romans 3:23).
2. God loves us and has a plan for us (John 10:10).
3. Repent of - that is to turn away from - our sins. We need to get them out of our lives, just like cleaning our spiritual houses (Romans 6:23).
4. Accept the fact that Jesus died to take our sins on Himself that we might receive forgiveness for them (John 3:16; Romans 5:8).
5. Actually make the decision to accept Him as Lord and Savior (John 14:6; Acts 4:12; John 1:12; Ephesians 2:8,9).

All of the members of the United Methodist Church need to truly accept Jesus Christ as Lord and Savior: laity, clergy, and bishops.

The Authority of the Bible

Our second need is to accept the authority of the Bible as God's word. This is interrelated with the first in that Jesus testifies to the truth of the Bible, and the Bible points to the sovereignty of Christ as Lord and Savior. Concurrently, the Bible must be central to our spiritual authority in our individual lives, homes, and church.

Architectural Changes Needed for Revival

1. The focus of ministry needs to be the local church. We need to recognize that this is the basic field of outreach in our denomination and is the UMC's main interface to the secular world.

2. The prioritization of ministry needs to be from the local to the general church (a "bottom-up" as opposed to a "top-down" philosophy). Requirements should originate at the local church. In that vein, all other elements of the UMC's structure should support the local church in its ministry. This means that a main function of the bishop is to facilitate each of his district superintendents in

their functions of supporting the pastors in the ministries of their local churches.

3. In the local church the function of the pastor should be to provide biblically spiritual nurture to his congregation, which should be considered a sacred trust from God.

4. Title to the property of a local church needs to be held by the local church. When a church building is constructed, financed, and cared for by the people in a congregation, they should own it.

5. The UMC's bureaucracies need to be downsized to the minimal functional level and commensurate with the support it receives from freewill offerings. One example is the huge GBGM staff that outnumbers the total full-time UM overseas missionary force. Brazilian Methodists took a radical step in their church, getting rid of most of the overhead it supported and almost "starting over."[1] We need to.

6. Stewardship. The mandatory apportionment should be eliminated in favor of the voluntary, biblical offering. Pressure and coercion to give should never be used to compel people to contribute against their better judgment as specified in 2 Corinthians 9:7. Some laity hesitate to give because of misuse of money. Churches should recognize their "first benevolent responsibility" is to pay the apportionment, but there is a prior responsibility for responsible spiritual leadership in the institution of the United Methodist Church. Since employees insist on concentrating money and activities on sociopolitical priorities, then people should be freed from the compulsion of giving through the mandatory apportionment, because use of that money violates their consciences.

7. Accountability. If our denominational employees and leaders will not abide by the Bible and the *Book of Discipline*, and will not provide leadership to ensure maintenance of the connection, they should not expect local churches and individuals to feel obligated to support their activities through the apportionment, voluntary or

otherwise. The laity have the right to provide practical, uncoerced support wherever they wish, and to not support what they view as defective spiritual leadership with their offerings - because the money belongs to the Lord, not to any man-made institution.

In conclusion, we have examined just some of the "malignant tumors" that are problems in our denomination; it has been unpleasant, but necessary. 2,379,976 people have left our church over the past twenty nine years. They are gone. Their money is gone and is working elsewhere. But if they had stayed, been a voice for truth, worked for revival, and contributed their money for that purpose in informing others as to what is happening, we would have a different denomination today. If the 2,379,976 people who left had used their money for the Lord to bring renewal to our denomination, we would have a different United Methodist Church today!

Note:
1. *Go, General Conference!* by Rev. Larry Eisenberg, Tulsa, OK; p. 43.

Closing Remarks

In December of 1979, as a young army officer experienced in the Vietnam war and the potential battlefields of Europe, I stood before a room full of senior military officers and civilians as I was briefing Major General William J. Hilsman, who was known to have a volatile temper. The subject of my analysis was that of battlefield communications, the doctrine espoused by General Hilsman's own command. I could have remained silent and not incurred the ire of some very powerful people in the room that day, but I preferred to risk my career to bring to their attention the fallacies of the system as it existed. To have remained silent might have meant the lives of countless soldiers, should the Soviets have unleashed their tanks, artillery, and aircraft against our outnumbered forces. The efficacy of those recommendations to streamline battlefield communications can be seen in the results of Operation Desert Storm, the last significant military effort in which I participated. The risk that I took paled in comparison to the fact that the battle was won and lives were saved.

How much more important to the eternal futures of countless souls is it for us to set aside any risk in our professional careers and personal lives to clearly communicate the saving message of Jesus Christ, while combating the forces of secularism that threaten to take over our United Methodist Church? Corporately, we must do this if our denomination is to have a viable future as a Christian institution.

South Georgia

....I was thinking as to how I might respond to his question, "Why should I stay?" I always invite the "hard" challenges when I speak, but his was very direct. Finally, I glanced at him and then spoke to the congregation as a whole:

"Think back to the beginnings of Methodism. One man, who had his heart warmed and entered a "Million Dollar Relationship" with Jesus Christ had a burning desire to save souls. A by-product of his concern for the welfare of others was helping them resolve their physical and social needs as well. Through his efforts, British society was transformed in such a way that the improvements prevented the revolution that devastated France. When Methodism came to the New World, it was a civilizing force in the development of our country. As the frontier swept westward, Methodist circuit riders took the gospel message to settlers and lives were changed. During those times, if you were to go into a village and find two churches, the chances were good that one would be Methodist. Methodism came to be known as "America's church." All of this through the efforts of just one man who had a life-changing experience with Jesus Christ - John Wesley.

Now think about today. What if we could, by some miracle, change the 8.5 million members of the United Methodist Church into 8.5 million John Wesleys. What would happen? We would turn this country upside down for Jesus Christ! Do you know the problems we are having with declining morality? As lives were changed, these would disappear, and our society would be rejuvenated. It wouldn't stop at our borders, but would erupt out of our country. We would have United Methodists taking the message of Jesus Christ all over the world - and you would see the world changed! Think about it."

Yes, just think about it!

That is why the United Methodist Church is worth fighting for.

Appendix A

Membership in the United Methodist Church

One area of concern for those of us in Concerned Methodists is the continuing loss of members from our United Methodist Church over the past twenty nine years - 2,379,976, or an average of 82,068 people per year, 6,839 per month, 1,579 per week, or 225.6 per day, for every one of those years. The yearly summary is as follows:

Year	Membership	Net Loss
1969	10,789,624*	First Year Tracked by CM+
1970	10,671,774*	117,850
1971	10,509,198*	162,576
1972	10,334,521*	174,677
1973	10,063,060*	271,461
1974	9,957,710*	105,350
1975	9,861,028*	96,682
1976	9,785,534*	75,494
1977	9,731,781*	53,753
1978	9,653,711*	78,070
1979	9,584,771*	68,940
1980	9,519,407*	65,364

Year	Membership	Net Loss
1981	9,457,012*	62,395
1982	9,405,164*	51,848
1983	9,332,712*	72,452
1984	9,266,853*	65,859
1985	9,192,172*	74,681
1986	9,124,575*	67.597
1987	9,055,145*	69,430
1988	8,979,139*	76,006
1989	8,904,824*	74,315
1990	8,849,538*	55,286
1991	8,785,184*	64,354
1992	8,723,034*	62,150
1993	8,646,466*	76,568
1994	8,584,199	62,267
1995	8,534,891	49,308
1996	8,492,130 (est.)	42,761 (est.)#
1997	8,448,125 (est.)	44,005 (est.)#
1998	8,409,648 (est.)	38,477 (est.)@

Notes:
*   Source of these figures is the General Minutes of the Annual Conferences of The United Methodist Church, General Council on Finance and Administration, Evanston, Illinois, 1969-1993.
+   1969 is the first year that is being tracked by Concerned Methodists.
#   This figure is estimated as closely as possible. We encountered difficulty in getting figures from six annual conferences for 1996 and two for 1998 due to a variety of problems. In one instance, a significant number of churches in the Yellowstone Conference delayed turning in their figures until after their annual conference was held. After that, the accuracy of their figures was problematic.
@   The Oklahoma Indian Missionary Conference didn't report its numbers, and 77 Western Pennsylvania pastors failed to turn in membership data on time. (United Methodist News Service #365)

Appendix B

The Methodist Syndrome

by Philip K. Shriver

I love my small community United Methodist Church. Our congregation would be considered more elderly than youthful or middle-aged—a characteristic probably common to most of our smaller churches today. They are a caring, compassionate group of Christians. Within their limited resources, they support their local church, and conscientiously, if somewhat dubiously, strive to provide their share of financial giving for apportionments and mission outreach.

When I look at my church in relation to the whole United Methodist Church with its seemingly infinite bureaucracy and controversial direction, we seem comfortably far removed, but I know we, and many thousands of churches like us, are, in reality, the understructure supporting the sprawling entity that the whole world views as the United Methodist Church. I don't really want to be seen as a part of that church. I want to be seen as a part of my church. And therein lies the problem facing so many of us today. It's a problem that should not exist, and would not exist but for my generation's blind faith in all things labeled Methodist.

We were, for the most part, born Methodists; belonged to the Epworth League; supported real, live Methodist missionaries; listened to Biblical preaching; and really experienced a great joy in the church culminating at Christmas and Easter. God and Country was more than a Scouting award earned through great effort. The words went together like meat and potatoes. Fourth of July and Armistice Day services were gems of oratory blending our spiritual and nation-heritage. No questions existed on matters of World Service expenditures. The Methodist missionaries who received the congregation's outreach dollars visited the church and talked to us about how our money was serving God. Methodist missionaries seemed to be everywhere.

Beyond a loyalty to America, we didn't know our pastor's political views. More importantly, we didn't care. They came to us only as spiritual leaders, counselors, and friends—responsibilities prayerfully undertaken and well-met.

We considered ourselves, basically, a conservative, evangelical church, and were so judged by the rest of society. Being Methodist was as natural as being French, or English, or German, or any other nationality or combination of nationalities.

Such was the church background of the middle-aged core of the Methodist Church when traditional mores began to crumble. The first readily recognizable signs of change appeared in the early sixties. We were made uneasy with newspaper stories invariably depicting the Methodist Church out on the liberal/left fringe with some, for us, rather alarming companions. We lulled ourselves with the knowledge that these news items concerned only actions taken by selected committees or commissions within the church bureaucracy. We were, after all, the real Methodist Church—the conservative, evangelical Methodist Church.

One-quarter of a century later, most of us still remain, still call ourselves Methodists, still live in another time, and still will not face the fact that our church is fast disappearing. Some of our number, perhaps more discerning than us, departed, seeking in other denominations, what we once were. Our youth left in droves, my own six children among them. Some of us stayed in defiance of what we perceived was happening. Some of us simply found it easier to stay than to go. But most of all, we stayed because from time long past, we were Methodist as surely as we were American.

If ever a silent majority should have made a noise, it was during the past twenty-five years in our own church. With our silence, we gave tacit approval to the direction our church was taking. Worse, with our money, we supported the hierarchy and financed their experimentations with contractual missionary work, liberation theology, and political activism. Now, our time is short. When we have gone, the last visage of that Methodist Church we remember will be gone with us. If that is good, then we should continue to be silent and generous. If, however, the old ways are worthy of return, we should stop biting our tongues and speak out.

I have noted that whenever I have taken exception, through whatever avenue was open to me, of the official United Methodist position on any one of many controversial issues, members whose thoughts I would never have guessed, speak quietly to me of their general agreement of my assessment. That's encouraging to know, but speaking quietly among ourselves will not change the direction of those who make policy in the church. Start with your minister. He/she deserves to know how you feel about the church's involvement in politics, protest marches, boycotts, strikes, and civil disobedience. Tell them how you feel about our official affinity to liberation theology. (If the term is unfamiliar to you, go to the public library.) Tell them if you would be more at ease giving to Methodist missionaries than to the National Council of Churches of Christ. Tell them if you think the Bible is fine without rewriting.

Then begin to write. Write to your District Superintendent, your Conference, your Bishop, and the Methodist publications. Write action items for your Annual Conference. Make your ideas and your presence felt. You are regularly asked by various church-affiliated groups to write letters to your congressional delegation and the President on political issues. How much more important is it to reclaim your church? The same strategies that moved the church to the left with a minority of members can return it with a majority membership more inclined to the middle of the road.

No great organizations, be they business empires or churches, can exist without funds. "Money talks" is a truism at the highest reaches of the United Methodist Church just as well as it is in the boardrooms of our great corporations.

You have every right to expect your giving to the church to be used in a manner consistent with your personal beliefs on how it can best do the Lord's will. Since the physical and spiritual needs of our world far surpass our abilities to meet them, no reason exists for the support of controversial, politically motivated causes. If you must, make your giving your voice. If your protests go unanswered or ignored, explore new channels for your giving. God is served in many ways. Never lessen your giving, and always support the local church, but you might find apportionments, other than Ministerial Support, less attractive than in the past. For example, you might be more comfortable with the Mission Society for United Methodists than with the NCCC through World Service. There are many avenues of giving to the Lord's work outside the official United Methodist Church. Ironically, using them might bring the church back closer to its Wesleyan foundations.

We oldsters are a very significant force within the church, and if we choose to flex our muscle, there is no question that we can bring back United Methodist evangelism dedicated to combating today's secularism rather than striving to co-exist.

Appendix C

Nicaragua - A Case Study

An article in the January 13, 1989 issue of *The United Methodist Reporter* says in bold letters "UM BISHOPS PLAN MISSION TO NICARAGUA." The article goes on to say "that eighteen United Methodist bishops from the United States, East Germany, and the Philippines... will spearhead a 'mission for peace' in Nicaragua... Objectives of the meeting are:

-'To witness the call of Jesus Christ for peace and justice, freedom and self-determination;

-'To be in solidarity with the people of Nicaragua and Central America in their aspirations for a decent life through the sharing of the gospel;

-'To reflect the legitimate urgency for peace, the factors that hinder this process and consequently take the necessary steps to assure its total implementation." Bishops who were to attend were: "Ernest T. Dixon, San Antonio, Texas, president of the United Methodist Council of Bishops; Elias Galvan, Phoenix, Ariz.; Lloyd T. Knox, Birmingham, Ala.; C. P. Minnick, Raleigh, NC.; Melvin G. Talbert, San Francisco; Neil L. Irons, Pennington, N.J.; Joseph H. Yeakel, Silver Spring, Md.; J. Woodrow Hearn, Lincoln, Neb. ; Kenneth W. Hicks, Topeka, Kan.; Robert C. Morgan, Jackson, Miss.; Paul A Granadosin, Baguio City, Philippines; W.T. Handy Jr., St. Louis; Leroy C. Hodapp, Indianapolis; Ruediger R. Minor, Dresden, East Germany; Felton E. May, Harrisburg, Pa.; Rueben P. Job, Des Moines, Iowa; Jack M Tuell, Los Angeles; and Woodie W. White, Springfield, Ill."(1)

The article goes on to say that "three of the United Methodist bishops-Dixon, Minnick, and Hicks-were members of a nine-member, United Methodist fact-finding delegation to Nicaragua in 1985.

After Bishop C.P. Minnick's return from Central America, he had a glowing report of Nicaraguan communists building "a model society for Central America."(2) Later the Council of Bishops registered their 'strong protest' against U.S. support of contra activity that they said was bringing 'torture, terror, and death to many innocent civilians."

The bishops also protested President Reagan's trade embargo and urged him and the U.S. Congress to open discussions with Nicaragua "seeking a negotiated, non-violent settlement of issues of conflict that threaten peace between the two countries." The article finishes with "Expressing concern for human rights, the delegates called on the U.S. Government to recognize the conflict in that region as struggles for human rights and self-determination rather than confrontations between the superpowers of East and West."(3) It should be noted that Dr. Kalmin D. Smith, who is a labor specialist for the Michigan House of Representatives and President of the Lansing District Council of Ministries, visited Nicaragua from October 17-28, 1984 under the auspices of the Board of Global Ministries; in his report "Observations of the Central America Trip" he was highly critical of the lack of objectivity of the trip. Dr. Smith wrote on page five of his report "Many Sandinista leaders told us that the revolution in Nicaragua should not be viewed as part of the East-West conflict."(4) This idea, originally expounded by Sandinista leaders, was the same one put forth to us by our bishops when they returned from their trip. It is doubtful that this was the bishops' original idea, yet it was given to us as their analysis of the situation.

These people, fourteen of whom were American United Methodist bishops-a third of the total here in the States-subsequently spent a week in Nicaragua, where there is not a single United' Methodist church. They went to Managua and proclaimed, "We will demand and expect that our government act with compassion and justice.

"We will publicly challenge our governments to be peacemakers and not peacebreakers.... We will work for the sovereign rights of other nations to govern themselves without interference." They went on to say, "We are here to express our joy for what the

Nicaraguan people have accomplished in their long struggle for self-determination and justice."

The Institute for Religion and Democracy (IRD) best introduces the analysis of the grandiloquent pronouncements of these bishops: "Joy? Accomplishments? These self-appointed prophets are not speaking the whole truth. They know there is no basis for joy, only tears."(5) To portray reality, a collection of events in Nicaragua is as follows:

-A teacher earns $12.00 per month; various estimates of the average wage range from $7.50 to $10.00 per month, down from the pre-Sandinista figure of $100.00 per month.

-There are between 7,000 and 10,000 political prisoners, according to Catholic bishop Bosco Vivas.

-The Catholic radio station is prohibited from giving the news (Vivas).

-La Prensa, the country's only truly independent newspaper, is heavily censored, and closed on an arbitrary basis. This is the same newspaper run by Jaime Chamorro, whose brother's murder on January 10, 1978 by Somoza henchmen precipitated the actions that ultimately resulted in the overthrow of the government. The Chamorro family, who has had four presidents in its history, came to oppose the Sandinistas when they failed to carry through on their promises of freedom and reform.

-Divine mobs("turbas divinas") regularly harass, terrorize, and beat, up politicians and others opposed to the government.

a. On July 24, 1982, Horacio Ruiz, a La Prensa editor, was forced into a car by four men-two with submachine guns-and taken to a remote place and beaten up.

b. Luis Mora Sanchez was locked in a cell with a gang and beaten up.

c. Alejandro Cordonero and Enrique Garcia, two reporters for La Prensa, were arrested, detained for fifteen days, and questioned about their activities on the newspaper. (6)

-Ration cards are confiscated for non-attendance at Sandinista rallies.

-In Chinandega, Daniel Ortega branded talk of inflation as "counter revolutionary." He stated that a pound of beans could be bought for five cordobas; a man in the audience offered him five cordobas for a pound, and was arrested and taken off later that day.

-On May 1,1984, a May Day rally attended by thousands of workers, peasants and young people chanted slogans like "El frente y Somoza son la misma cosa. (The Sandinistas and Somoza are the same thing)." (7)

-On June 26, 1986, La Prensa was closed. (8)

-The Nicaraguan government executed 200 people it caught rummaging for food in a Managua dump. (9)

-During January-February, 1988, 15,000 workers marched during a massive protest in Managua against the Sandinista government. They demonstrated against food shortages and lack of government response to demands for improved economic, social, and political conditions.

-Inflation in 1988 was 22,500 percent.

-On January 23, 1989, Daniel Ortega said he was laying off 23,000 workers to cut a budget deficit.

-In May, 1989, 5,000 opposition supporters marched through the town of Masaya shouting, "Democracy Yes, Sandinismo No."(10)

Dr. Jaime Bengoechea, president of the Chamber of Industry and a pharmacist, stated, "We have a human tragedy in Nicaragua. Our society is disintegrating. When a country is abandoned by 16 percent of its people including 60 percent of its professional and technical people, that's a tragedy. A bottle of milk costs a half day's pay. A thousand companies have been expropriated. A circus visited here three years ago and had its tent confiscated as a 'public utility'! Can you imagine anyone investing here with that behavior?" (11)

A report by the Puebla Institute, a lay Catholic human rights organization, confirms the above mentioned information. It also regretted the massive exodus of people from Nicaragua. In interviews of people in refugee camps in Honduras and Costa Rica as described in its fifty-two page report entitled "Fleeing their Homeland", it gave the following reasons for fleeing their native country:

-Restriction on freedom of religion. "Religious activists suffered harassment and discrimination by the Nicaraguan government, including prohibitions on preaching, evangelizing, and attending prayer meetings.

-"Sandinista military attacks against civilians.... The attacks occurred indiscriminately and without warning.

-"Arbitrary arrest and detention... without due process as a method of harassment and intimidation.

-"Torture and ill treatment in detention. Among the methods used were severe beatings during interrogations, prolonged deprivation of food and/or water, and mock executions.

-"The military draft. Religious pacifists are given no opportunity for conscientious objector status in violation of their religious rights. " (12)

Yet, contrary to these and other sources of information on the state of affairs in Nicaragua, the Methodist bishops summarized

71

their thoughts in a signed statement entitled "A Declaration of Peace and Solidarity." This Declaration sharply contrasts with a pastoral letter that Nicaragua's Roman Catholic bishops released in June, 1988. It should be noted that all of the Methodist bishops live outside of Nicaragua; the Catholic bishops are all from Nicaragua. The Methodist bishops who traveled to Central America to investigate the "Nicaraguan reality," as they called it, came to completely different conclusions from those of the Catholic bishops, who are actually a part of the Nicaraguan reality, since they live there for 365 days a year, and are not there for just a five day visit. (13) The Methodist bishops state that "peace for these Central American nations is our deepest desire and our greatest hope," and go on to define peace in terms of Psalm 85, citing verses 10,11. They then assert that "peace with justice is possible in our time." From this point it is worthwhile to quote the analysis of the Religion and Society Report:

"The authors of the Methodist Declaration are convinced that the responsibility for achieving peace in Central America lies squarely on the shoulders of our governments." Again, the Declaration's prescriptions seem to assign no particular peacemaking responsibilities to the government of Nicaragua. That is rather unusual, since the Nicaraguan government has been engaged in a civil war-sometimes at high-intensity levels-since the demise of the Somoza regime. Therefore, it is reasonable to assume that if peace... is to be achieved in Central America today, it will require the full cooperation of the government of Nicaragua, as well as the cooperation of other governments in the Americas. The point is that peace in Central America cannot be premised on the notion that the government of Nicaragua is a defenseless victim of geopolitical realities and not a crucial political agent in its own right."

In sharp contrast to the Methodist bishops, the Catholic bishops address specific problems present in Nicaraguan society, but, significantly, begin on a note of martyrdom. The Nicaraguan government has for the past ten years conducted a war against the Catholic church by banning Catholic radio newscasts, expelling foreign priests on charges of treason, shut down Catholic social organizations, and as illustrated in the April 1986 Readers Digest article

"The Lonely Struggle of a Nicaraguan Priest," encouraged mob violence against the church and priests themselves. Nicaragua's Catholic bishops decry the economic deterioration, alienation, desperation, administrative deficiency, high military expenditure, and the "materialistic and atheistic education." In addition they criticize the so-called "people's churches" that combine the Christian faith with a materialistic ideology, and is controlled by the state; these provide the illusion of the government's cooperating in propagating religion. (16) In addition, the Nicaraguan Catholics lament many of the problems in the life of their society: the so called "trial marriages," abortion, increasing disunity of the family, alcoholism, "delinquency, sexual debauchery, violence, and amorality."

The fact that the Methodist bishops have decided to ignore the contents of the Catholic bishops' letter to present a favorable picture of the Sandinista government raises serious questions about their purpose in issuing their statement on Nicaragua in the first place. Again, to quote the Religion and Society Report, ".... the Methodist work and the Roman Catholic work are dramatically different. Though that is not surprising, it is disappointing for one basic reason. That reason is ecumenical in nature. It appears that the position of the Methodist bishops does not take seriously the concerns of the Roman Catholic bishops. By largely ignoring most of the expressed concerns of the Roman Catholic bishops of Nicaragua, the Methodist bishops might be understood to be neglecting their assigned duty to be leaders 'in the quest for Christian unity' (The Book of Discipline, 1988, p.284). The Methodist bishops call for their 'congregations to stand with the poor and the oppressed: to pray with them, share with ;them, and to suffer with them as the Gospel demands.' That call, which is certainly valid, would be authenticated by Methodism's bishops standing with the poor and oppressed Roman Catholic Church of Nicaragua, which is presently under the thumb of a Nicaraguan government that fears and thus perverts democratization."(14) This means that the Methodist bishops have ignored the concerns of the bishops of a fellow Christian religion in deference to a political government. That would constitute a political decision, and consequent political activism. Further, that government is a Marxist-Leninist government which is professedly atheistic. An all-important question is "Why are religious leaders of our church, nominally a Christian church, supporting an atheistic government and movement to the detriment of a fellow Christian movement?" That is a question that must be answered.

A review of the information contained in the summer, 1989 issue of The Christian Methodist Newsletter will quickly dispel the idea that Nicaragua is a defenseless victim of events in Central America: the picture of the Soviet-made 122mm multiple rocket launcher (MRL), the copies of the grade school math books that show Nicaraguan children are taught using Soviet AK-47 assault rifles and hand grenades, and the extreme anti-U.S., and revolutionary rhetoric shown on the Sandinista posters and in the interpretation of the Sandinista hymn. In addition, the two pages reproduced from the publication Soviet Military Power give the tonnages of military equipment shipped to Nicaragua over the space of several years, describing the types of weapons, the quantities, sources, and the progressively increasing amounts. This corresponds with the revelations contained in Major Roger Miranda Bengoechea's disclosures of Daniel Ortega's intentions: after having signed an agreement to bring peace to Central America in August, 1987, Ortega returned to Managua, convened a closed meeting of the National Assembly, and laid out his plan-"The peace plan is a weapon to eliminate the Contras. First, it should be used to influence the U.S. Congress to cut off funds to the Contras. Once that happened, the Contras would cease to exist. Then the Sandinistas would build active and reserve forces of 600,000 soldiers (remember, Nicaragua has a total population of 3 million people). By 1995 they would have received flame throwers, 122mm self-propelled howitzers, and a squadron of MiG 2lBs from the Soviets. This military might would help them establish a Soviet Central America."The Nicaraguan offensive against the United States also takes the form of massive drug shipments. Under the sponsorship of the Ministry of the Interior, and Tomas Borge in particular, it is designed to undermine and corrupt America from the inside. To use the words of Humberto Ortega, "It's a way of waging war on the United States. It also provides a profit."(15, 16, 17,18)

As shown previously, the Marxist war of revolution is not limited to Nicaragua alone: in February, 1988, a courier for the communist guerrillas in El Salvador was captured, and a number of important secret documents fell into our hands. One of these provided an extremely interesting picture of what is planned for the United States and for the countries of Central America. This document was evidently prepared for the guidance of the top guerrilla leaders in El Salvador. It observes that the surrender of the anticommunist freedom fighters in Nicaragua "will be a strategic defeat of the gravest importance for the United States." It says that this will have global impact, producing "a global strategic reversal." It predicts that this will help the efforts of the communist insurgents to overthrow the government of El Salvador. It declared the Arias peace plan for Nicaragua-in its own words-"was and will continue to be a positive political instrument for the revolution so long as the revolutionary forces use it offensively to divide and weaken the enemy. Now we have the advantage, the war (in El Salvador) will become more intense and soon will become the dominant one in Central America after the negotiation period." Subsequently, Robert Pear, diplomatic correspondent of The New York Times, pointed out that the new FMLN offensive was fueled by arms shipments from Nicaragua. Pear noted that although the Arias peace plan, signed by Daniel Ortega, committed Nicaragua to stop sending arms to the Salvadoran rebels, a truckload of arms being shipped from Nicaragua to El Salvador was intercepted in Honduras on October 18, 1989. It had included AK-47 assault rifles, 19,000 rounds of ammunition, and more than 500 rockets, detonators, and radios. The truck driver, under interrogation, admitted delivering weapons every month since August, 1988. Pear also reported that the five top FMLN commanders had been seen in Managua two weeks prior to the attack on San Salvador, (19)

The importance of the propaganda war to try to influence people in the United States into thinking that Nicaragua is harmless and constitutes no threat to the region nor to the security of the United States is best illustrated by a statement made by Daniel Ortega himself, "The real war for Nicaragua is being waged not in Nicaragua, but in the United States." Anyone with the least bit of knowledge and background about Marxist-Leninist theory, and the history of Central America can understand the sequence of events: they have been repeated over and over and over. I believe it was George Santayana who said, "Those who do not remember history are doomed to repeat it." Yet Bishop Ernest T. Dixon of San Antonio, Texas is outspoken in giving advice to the President on Central American Policy; a few weeks ago, Spurgeon M. Dunnam, III, Editor-General Manager of *The United Methodist Reporter*, waxed eloquent about America's failed policy in Central America. The information contained in this Newsletter is completely unclassified,taken from sources available to everyone, to include members of the Methodist clergy. The President has available to him the information from these same sources plus all of the intelligence gathering sources of the Nation at levels not available to the common people: For Official Use Only (FOUO), Confidential, Secret, and Top Secret. He is in a far better position to judge the true state of affairs in Central America, and more particularly, in Nicaragua and El Salvador. Yet Bishop Ernest T. Dixon, Bishop C.P. Minnick, and the other members of the clergy who presume to speak out on these issues, have evidently not availed themselves of even the basic sources of information used in *The Christian Methodist Newsletter*. Furthermore, had the bishops done their homework, they would have discovered that so called "fact finding tours" have long been used by communist countries as means of propaganda to influence people into supporting their causes; this technique pre-dates the 1917 communist revolution and has its origin in Czarist Russia. During Catherine the Great's 1787 tour of the newly annexed Crimean territories, her statesman and favorite Grigory Potemkin undertook elaborate measures to make this area appear to be wealthier and more populous than it was in reality. Among other things, he ordered several fake villages to be constructed along Catherine's route. The phrase "Potemkin village" has since then become a common designation of a fraud designed to deceive outsiders. (20) The question remains, "Why were the bishops so easily deceived?" Combined with the above information, it appears that there is a decided political bias common among the group. What else would explain the fact that they so strongly support the Marxist Nicaraguan government, which has never once been elected to power, and Oppose the Nicaraguan freedom fighters("Contras"), and yet in El Salvador they consistently oppose the democratically-elected government, and support the FMLN guerrillas, who are communists. Why do they oppose U.S. involvement in Central America, yet have said absolutely nothing about support given by the Eastern Block countries, which completely outstrips that provided by the United States in both dollars and manpower? They decry the 55 military advisory personnel in El Salvador yet say nothing about the 69,000 Warsaw Pact personnel in Nicaragua. These questions also need to be answered.

It is the position of Concerned Methodists that the public political pronouncements made by the bishops based on their "fact finding" trip to Central America are not credible. This study utilizing only a small percentage of information available on Nicaragua proves conclusively that the situation there has nothing whatsoever to do with "self-determination," and is nothing more than a buildup by the Soviet Union of a staging base for Marxist-style revolution throughout Central America. This our religious leaders have failed to grasp.

Our bishops and other church personnel consistently speak well of the Sandinistas, but what do the Sandinistas really think about them? After all, these well-meaning people travel all the way from the United States, take time out of their busy schedules, and spend church money to go to Nicaragua and get the whirlwind "Potemkin Tour." They then return to the States dedicated to work on behalf of the Sandinistas. Tomas Borge, the previously mentioned Interior Minister, chief of the Nicaraguan Secret Police, and head of their propaganda operation calls them "tontos utiles." This translates literally to "foolish useful ones," or more commonly "useful idiots."

That is a sad testimony on the leadership of our church - "useful idiots."

[Original signed in November, 1989 by]
Allen O. Morris, Chairman
Concerned Methodists

Notes:

1. *The United Methodist Reporter*, January 13, 1989.
2. *The Fayetteville Observer*, April 11, 1986, p. 5a.
3. *Reporter.*
4. Paper "Observations of the Central America Trip," by Dr. KalminD. Smith, p. 5.
5. *Religion and Democracy* newsletter, pub. by the IRD, March, 1989. p. 2.
6. "Our People Cannot Be Silenced," *Readers Digest* (RD), May, 1987.
7. "Disillusion in Nicaragua," Readers Digest, March, 1985.
8. "Silenced," p. 174.
9. *Notable Quotables*, pub. by MediaWatch, April 1, 1989, p. 1.
10. *The Fayetteville Times*, May 29, 1990, p. 2a.
11. *Religion and Democracy* newsletter, p. 2.
12. *Wichita Falls Record*, May 6, 1987, p. 13a.
13. *The Religion and Society Report*, June, 1989, p. 3.
14. Ibid., p. 4.
15. "High Stakes in Central America," David Reed, RD, Aug, 1983.
16. "Triple Threat to the Western Hemisphere," *Defense/86*, May/June 86, p. 7. This article was based on a speech by Hector D.Sanchez, Deputy Assistant Secretary of Defense (Inter-American Affairs) to the Council on Foreign Relations.
17. "On the Ramparts in Central America," *Army*, L. James Binder, ed. May, 1987.
18. Nicaragua's Secret Plan, by Trevor Armbrister, April, 1988.
19. *The AIM Report*, Accuracy in Media, November-B, 1989, p. 4.
20. *The Gulag Archipelago-Three*, Aleksander I. Solzhenitsyn, p, 537.

Appendix D

Timeline of the Sophia/"goddess" Theologies

Following is a Timeline for the goddess theologies that have become an influence in the United Methodist Church. Unless otherwise noted, all entries in this Timeline have been reprinted courtesy of Mr. Eric Umile of the JCL Task Force in the Eastern Pennsylvania Conference (EPC). This is not a comprehensive list; other events have occurred. For a more complete listing, review this on the Concerned Methodists' website at: http://www.fayetteville.com/concerned-methodists/

Mid- to late- 1970s. The Rev. Hal Taussig, pastor at Calvary UMC in Philadelphia, discovers that women in his congregation are dissatisfied with the predominance of male images of God. Taussig introduces them to the Biblical figure of Wisdom or "Sophia".

Early 1980s. Led by Rev. Taussig and the Rev. Susan A. Cady, several women at Calvary UMC start a Sophia study group. In 1983 they begin to experiment with the Gospel accounts, and replace Jesus' name with the name of Sophia.

March 10, 1984. Revs. Cady and Taussig lead a seminar entitled, "Who is Sophia?" at Arch Street UMC. Sister Marian Ronan also participates. The seminar is sponsored by the EPC Commission on the Status and Role of Women (COSROW).

1986. Revs. Cady and Taussig, together with Sr. Marian Ronan, publish their first book, *Sophia: The Future of Feminist Spirituality*. The book is dedicated to the Rev. Sandra Forrester Dufresne.

June, 1987. Bishop F. Herbert Skeete transfers Revs. Cady and Taussig from Calvary UMC to the Ridge Group Ministry in Roxborough.

February 13, 1989. An article in *Newsweek* entitled "Feminism and the Churches" states: "Putting more women in the pulpit is no longer the prime goal of Christian feminists. Rather, their aim is a thorough and comprehensive transformation of the language, symbols, and sacred texts of Christian faith - and therefore of the faith itself."

February 19, 1989. Front page article appears on *The Philadelphia Inquirer* entitled, "Women Creating Ritual to Fill a Religious Void." The article speaks of feminist theology and describes a "Sophia Eucharist" which took place in Rev. Cady's home in Germantown.

February 21, 1989. Eric M. Umile, lay leader at Emmanuel UMC, Roxborough, reads the Inquirer article. Disturbed by the news that his pastor is involved in goddess worship, he begins to investigate.

March, 1989. Umile reads *Sophia: The Future of Feminist Spirituality,* then addresses the issue of the book with his church's PPR Committee and northwest district superintendent Claude Edmonds. No feedback is given in either case. A discussion with his pastor, Susan Cady, leads to an impasse; she makes no mention of her upcoming new book.

Spring, 1989. Revs. Cady and Taussig establish "Sophia House", "an organization dedicated to education spiritually focused on the Biblical figure of Wisdom/Sophia." The organization has ties to the Daughters of Wisdom, a Roman Catholic order.

May 8, 1989. Date of Umile's letter to Bishop Susan Morrison with concern about the Cady/Taussig book; he asks for episcopal leadership.

May 25, 1989. Bishop Morrison responds, saying she has not read the book yet affirms the ministry of its authors, saying, "Our church is blessed in its openness to new "theological perspectives."

July 12, 1989. Harper and Row publishes *Wisdom's Feast: Sophia in Study and Celebration,* an expanded edition of Cady, Ronan, and Taussig's earlier book. The publishers describe [the] book as follows: "This practical handbook combines theory and practice of the worship of Sophia in one indispensable volume, introducing her importance to Christian feminist spirituality." (*Harper's Torch Letter*, May 90). It contains litanies, a Eucharist, prayers, liturgies, and steps for introducing "Sophia" theology into church practice. Sophia is "a goddess that reigns coequally with God," but knowledge of her has been suppressed by "patriarchy," which is a "demonic aspect of classical Western spirituality." Sophia replaces Jesus in portions of rewritten scriptures, "walking on water toward her disciples", etc. Christianity is "patriarchal in spirit, and, hence, unacceptable and dangerous to the feminist cause."

"Fairest Sophia, Ruler of all nature,
     O Thou in whom earth and heav'n are one,
Thee will I cherish, thee will I honor,
     Thou, my soul's glory, joy, and crown."

- From an actual review of the book *Wisdom's Feast* itself by Allen O. Morris.

October 5, 1989. An article on *Wisdom's Feast* written by Eric Umile entitled "Why silence about heresy?" is published in the UM Reporter.

October 27, 1989. A rebuttal by Sandra Forrester Dufresne appears in *the UM Reporter,* defending Revs. Cady and Taussig.

November 24, 1989. Umile writes to Bishop Jack Tuell, President of the Council of Bishops, stating his concerns about *Wisdom's Feast.*

November 27, 1989. Bishop Tuell responds to the Umile letter, saying he has not read the book and that the Council of Bishops exercises no authority over individual bishops.

December, 1989. Robert Grow, a member of Emmanuel UMC, Roxborough, writes to Bishops Morrison and Tuell stating his concerns.

December 15, 1989. Bishop Morrison responds to the Grow letter. "I have received your letter of concern about statements made and books written by the Rev. Susan Cady. At this point, I have not had a chance to read the books, thus am not really in a position to respond."

December 15, 1989. Bishop Tuell responds to Grow letter: "This is a matter which needs to be dealt with in the [EPC]."

Winter, 1990. The Lay Coalition For Doctrinal Integrity (LCDI) is organized by United Methodists in the Roxborough area for the purpose of "educating the EPC about *Wisdom's Feast.*

April 1, 1990. LCDI sends 4-page letter to all EPC lay leaders, informing them about *Wisdom's Feast.*

April 24, 1990. LCDI submits resolution 9023 to the EPC denouncing *Wisdom's Feast* as incompatible with the Christian faith and asking Bishop Morrison to state the official position of the EPC on the book.

June 9, 1990. EP Annual Conference: Bishop Morrison rules Resolution 9023 out of order, saying she does not rule on positions for the EPC.

July/August, 1990. Of LCDI's efforts, Bishop Morrison is quoted as saying: "People have a right to be concerned about what is written..."

January 15-17, 1991. Hal Taussig speaks at the Winter Convocation on Ministry, sponsored by the EPC Board of Ordained Ministry...on modern liturgical evolution, especially through the use of images of Sophia.

February 1-3, 1991. Revs. Cady and Taussig lead seminar, "An Introduction to Sophia: Wisdom Ways" at Kirkridge Retreat Center.

March 9, 1991. In accordance with resolution 9022, the EPC's Theological Issues Task Force holds a forum on *Wisdom's Feast* at Holy Cross UMC in Reading. Audience's questions to presenters are screened by forum moderators. Discussion is limited to small groups. The question of the compatibility of Sophia worship...is not addressed.

April 9, 1991. Writing to V.E. Maybray of the Mission Society for United Methodists, Bishop Morrison says of *Wisdom's Feast*, "I understand the book to be exploratory theology not doctrine." She expresses concern about the "divisive negative energy [on] the issue."

April 15, 1991. Bishop Morrison writes episcopal letter to the EPC clergy offering reassurances of her responsiveness to the *Wisdom's Feast* issue, and wondering why UMs are spending "valuable time attacking and condemning each other within the Community of Faith." She gives assurances that Sophia theology is not taught in local churches, and recommends channeling the time and energy around the issue into more "positive steps".

May 6, 1991. An article in Time magazine entitled, "When God was a Woman" maintains that worshipers of Mother Earth are part of a goddess resurgence. The article states, "A book by two [UM] pastors proposes experimental Bible readings about the crucifixion that replace Jesus with Sophia (Wisdom), a name...used by Goddess-minded Christians."

May, 1991. Forums are held by JCLTF and MFSA, who distribute literature. The Daughters of Wisdom Order holds a dialogue session.

June 14-15, 1991. Western Pennsylvania Annual Conference (WPC) petition P35 reaffirms United Methodism's doctrinal positions and denounces *Wisdom's Feast* as "contrary to the doctrinal standards of the UM Church and the plain teachings of Scripture." It is adopted and referred to the 1992 General Conference for adoption. WPC petition P36 asks the Northeastern Jurisdictional Committee on the Episcopacy for a report on the facts of the Wisdom's Feast matter and how it was resolved by Bishop Morrison. This petition is also adopted.

July 1, 1991. Bishop Morrison appoints Sandra Forrester Dufresne as district superintendent of the Lebanon-Reading district.

November 30, 1991. Susan Cady leads workshop, "Wisdom Ways: An introduction to Sophia" at a 3-day seminar entitled, "Celebrating Women in Ministry," sponsored by FUMC of Germantown in cooperation with COSROW. Bishop Morrison is a principal speaker at the seminar.

January 14, 1992. The Northeast Jurisdictional Committee on the Episcopacy responds to the WPC's petition (P36), saying that it is not a disciplinary function of the committee to investigate the Sophia controversy or Bishop Morrison's handling of it.

March, 1992. The JCLTF sends 3 petitions to General Conference: 1. calls for reaffirmation of UM doctrinal standards; 2. calls for an investigation of Sophia theology; 3. calls for mechanisms to hold pastors and seminaries accountable for what they teach and preach.

May 15, 1992. General Conference: WPC resolution P35 (adopted on June 14, 1991) is defeated. The three JCLTF petitions disappeared.

June, 1992. EP Annual Conference: JCLTF's resolution 9225 asking Bishop Morrison and the cabinet to clarify their position of

Wisdom's Feast is defeated 346-250. Susan Cady is elected as vice-chairperson of the Board of Ordained Ministries, and chairperson of the Joint Review Committee (which oversees grievance procedures).

January 4,1993, The Rev. Mark Rains, an EPC pastor working independently, files a grievance against *Wisdom's Feast* at Bishop Morrison's Valley Forge office.

April, 1993. The EPC mediation team reportedly reaches the conclusion that *Wisdom's Feast* is a scholarly work dealing with speculative theology and there is no grounds to pursue further action against the authors of the book. Rev. Rains contends that the matter has not been settled or the two parties reconciled to each other. Nevertheless, Bishop Morrison will not move the grievance to a complaint.

June 7, 1993. EPAC: A resolution submitted by Glenside UMC calling for Bishop Morrison to repudiate Sophia worship is tabled.

July 19, 1993. In a letter to a member of Glenside UMC, Bishop Morrison states that the Rains grievance was "processed to a mediation team but will not go any further."

August, 1993. An article appears in *Christianity Today* entitled "Encountering the goddess at Church." Written by Dr. Thomas C. Oden, the article describes a Holy Communion service which took place at the Theological School at Drew University. The service was led by a "highly visible feminist leader" identified as Susan Cady....During the service, the hymn "Sophia" was followed by...an invitation to commune, not in the Lord's name, but in Sophia's name.

October 6, 1993. Rev. Mark Rains mails research document to EPC clergy and to active and retired Bishops. In a cover letter, Rev. Rains writes: "Unfortunately, (Bishop Morrison) has decided not to move his grievance to a complaint. After much prayer..., I must now inform you that I am...filing a grievance against Bishop Morrison."

November 4-7, 1993. "Re-Imagining" Conference is held at Minneapolis in recognition of the Ecumenical Decade of Churches in Solidarity with Women (an initiative of the World Council of Churches). Sophia is...worshiped at a service of milk and honey, and the "miracle of being lesbian, out, and Christian" is celebrated. The doctrine that God and humanity are reconciled through Christ's death on the cross is downgraded...Some 405 Presbyterians and 391 United Mehodists attend the event, including Bishop Susan Morrison. The Women's Division of the General Board of Global Ministries calls "Re-Imagining" its major theological workshop of the 1992-1996 quadrennium.

- RENEW, the evangelical UM Women's network, and personal interviews with conference attendees (Mrs. Dottie Chase, Ms. Susan Cyre, and Mrs. Kathy Kersten) by Allen O. Morris.

January 3-6, 1994. At the Congress on Evangelism in Myrtle Beach, SC, retired UM Bishop Earl G. Hunt states that the Christian worship of Sophia is a heresy that "staggers the religious mind." He also says, "No comparable heresy has appeared in the church in the last 15 centuries." Bishop Hunt calls upon active UM bishops to act...to eradicate Sophia worship from the Church.

- The United Methodist Reporter

January, 1994. In a prepared statement, Ms. Joyce Sohl, chief executive officer at the Women's Division (WD) of the GBGM, denies that it was an official sponsor or funder of the "Re-Imagining" event (However, the conference's own handbook lists the Women's Division as a funder). In addition, from the RENEW network, we have: "1. The decision of the Women's Division to fund the attendance of any staff members or directors whose schedules would allow attendance showed a willingness to make a substantial financial commitment. Thirty-six directors, nine staff members and eleven United Methodist Women conference vice presidents attended, all expenses paid, according to the 'Fact Sheet' released by the Women's Division. Connie Takamine, Treasurer of the Women's Division, has indicated that the total cost for these attendees was $35,081. 2. In addition, a grant of $2,500 was given

to the Minnesota Conference United Methodist Women for the 'Global Theological Conference Re-Imagining.' The Women's Division has indicated that this grant was for Minnesota scholarships."
- RENEW, the evangelical coalition for United Methodist Women's

January/February, 1994. *The Presbyterian Layman* magazine condemns the use of $66,000 in Presbyterian funds for the "Re-Imagining" Conference. The headline lead article reads: "Declaring their allegiance to the goddess 'Sophia', participants...heralded a more radical agenda: to promote a new religion with a new god."
- *The Presbyterian Layman*, January/February, 1994.

February, 1994. Joyce Sohl and Carolyn Johnson of the WD of the GBGM mail a "video letter" to all conference and district UMWs in which they discuss the importance of attending ecumenical gatherings. As for the flap over Sophia worship, Dr. Johnson expresses her trust in the ability of UM women to discern diverse theology for themselves.
- RENEW, the evangelical coalition for United Methodist Women; the video "A Time of Hope, A Time of Threat"

Spring. 1994. A religion course (REL 485) taught at Methodist College, Fayetteville, NC, features books entitled *When God was a Woman* and *The Once and Future Goddess* with themes of goddess worship and pantheism. Books given to Concerned Methodists by the irate parent of a Methodist College student.[The family left the UMC and joined a Baptist Church.]

April 9, 1994. The Miriam Conference held in Urbana, Illinois featured goddess worship, pantheism, and New Age beliefs. On pages 2 and 3 of the Spoken Litany were:
SIDES: in the breaking of the waters when life comes forth from the womb, your gift of life and love...
Leader: Eternal One, we need your living water here today. May the water from Miriam's well return to your people...
ALL: God our Mother, Living Water, River of Mercy, Source of Life, in whom we live, and move, and have our being,... be for

us always a fountain of life.... Honor and blessing, glory and praise to You forever. Amen.

In the Acknowledgments section, listed at the top was: "Sponsor: Baker Board, Ministry with Women; Wesley Foundation...."

This comment was placed on the same page:
"The Re-Imagining Conference held in Minneapolis, Minnesota in November, 1993 has become a subject of controversy within some denominations. Those of us on the Baker Board who attended the Re-Imagining Conference want to witness to the positive influence this event has been in our lives and to acknowledge the contribution of the conference to the shape and feel of today's program."
- From the program bulletin. The litany is from "Women prayer, Women Song: Resources for Ritual" by Miriam Therese Winter."

"During the Litany, another woman came to the table, took the water from one of the pitchers and poured it out completely into the large bowl on the table. While she was doing this rather slowly everyone except Virginia and I, said the following prayer: 'God our Mother, Living Water, River of Mercy, Source of Life, in whom we live, and move, and have our being, who quenches our thirst, refreshes,...Honor and blessing, glory and praise to You forever. Amen.'"

During her time of preaching, she said, 'The Bible is not a rule book of what we should or should not do.' 'The Bible is born in patriarchy, there should be a caution label on it saying, 'Caution, reading this could be dangerous to your health and survival.'...'
- Letter from one of the attendees at the "Miriam Conference" dated April 11, 1994; program of the event itself.

June 4, 1994. "People Keeping Faith with Creation" in Western New York State features pantheism and New Age beliefs.

August, 1994. The North Carolina Conference summer school held at Methodist College offers books authored by "Re-Imagining" speakers. In the UMW mission theme "Glimpses of God, Reflections of Christ" we find ideas from the "Re-Imagining"

Conference. Under the title "Naming the Holy One" "The naming of God is a sacred act; the words we use give meaning to our imagining of the Divine..." In addition, a litany quoted by the class "Biblical Concepts of Family," alternatively refers to God as being in "everyman, hanging on street corners, tasting the grace of cheap wine and the sting of the needle, who is pregnant without husband, who is child without parent, who has no place to play, who can't read nor write, who is on welfare and who is treated like garbage,...whose belly is huge and whose clothes burst with the new life, cares for her children at night and dreams of better days, and is alone...." - Conference material.

October 12-13, 1994. HEARTSOUNDS forum, held in Cambridge, Ohio, features goddess worship, pantheism, auto-eroticism, and lesbianism themes. Delores Williams is a featured speaker, and a bibliography of suggested resources included *Wisdom's Feast, She Who Is, and Called into Her Presence.* - A flyer on the event itself

October 29 1994. A "Re-Imagining Reunion" is held in Minneapolis sponsored by a permanent, non-profit group called the "Re-Imagining Community." *Re-Imagining*, its first quarterly newsletter is published.

December 28, 1994 - January 1, 1995. A Bible study for college students, held at St. Louis, Missouri with Rita N. Brock and Edwina Gateley as featured speakers, received $10,500 UM support. Gateley, [stated] "A big God is black and white and brown and yellow and gay and straight." She is the author of *A Warm Moist Salty God: Women Journeying Towards Wisdom.*

February, 1995. Re-Imagining Community's second newsletter Re-Imagining subtitled "Re-Imagining: Body and Soul" is published.

February 18, 1995. Joyce Sohl, keynote speaker for the "Re-Imagining Revisited" meeting at St. Lukes UMC in Oklahoma City, Oklahoma named her address "Goals of the Re-Imagining Conference."

May 4, 1995. A "Service of the Word" is held at UM-related Garrett-Evangelical Theological Seminary. It included a service at the chapel of the Unnamed Faithful in which the following words were repeated by seminary students as an act of worship:

- People: 0 Prehistoric Goddess, reveal to us Your names so we can call You when we need You.
- Caller: Who are You, 0 Holy One? How have Your daughters named You?
- Voice: I am Ishtar and Inanna....
- Voice: I am Isis of Egypt, manifest wisdom, eye of Re the sun god, Universal Goddess.
- People: Isis, show us Wisdom in everything and in everyone.
- Voice: I am Hathor, Egypt's Golden One. Look for me in the sycamore. Look for Me in the sky.
- Voice: I am Cybele, Great Mother goddess of ancient Anatolia.
- People: Fill us, Cybele, Great Mother Goddess, with your long lived nurturing Spirit.
- Voice: I Am Nut of the sky, of Egypt, Goddess of Affection.
- People: Nut, we call upon your name and long for Your affection.
- Voice: I am Anath-Astarte, and Lady Asherah of the Sea.
- "LANGUAGE", *The Evangelist*, May/June, 1995; published by Rick Bonfirm Ministries.

August 7-11, 1995. At the UM Clergywomen's Consultation in Atlanta, Miriam Therese winter used "Sophia," "Shekinah," and "Shaddai" as synonyms for God and refers to God as "She." She also invited the 800 women to sing to the tune of "Swing Low! Sweet Chariot" "Sing lo! Sing oh, Sophia! Wisdom come abide in my heart."

September 4 - 15, 1995. The UN Fourth World Conference on Women features seminars such as "Lesbian Activism from an Interfaith Perspective"; "Women, Religion, & Culture"; "Goddess and Women Hand in Hand"; and "Religion and Culture - Force for Women" which offered the story of a woman who left her Catholic faith to find "...joy as a wiccan." The Women's Environment and

Development Organization (WEDO), headed by Bella Abzug, and funded in part by the UM Women's Division, sponsored..."Daughters of the Earth." The first session was dedicated to the Chinese goddess Nu Kwa....Subsequent programs were dedicated to goddesses such as Songi, Athena, Tara, Pasowee, Ishtar, Ixmucane, Aditi, and Nanshe.

- The Institute on Religion and Democracy

1995 - 1996. Increased use in UM circles of books such as *Seasons of the Feminine Divine* by Mary Kathleen Speegle Schmitt, *In Memory of Her* by Elisabeth Schussler Fiorenza, and *Jesus, Miriam's Child, Sophia's Prophet* also by Fiorenza. This last book contains statements such as "By naming Jesus as the child of Miriam and the prophet of Divine Sophia, I seek to create a 'women' - defined feminist theoretical space that make it possible to dislodge christological discourse from their malestream frame of reference."[emphasis added]

October 5, 1996. "Accessing the Divine Light." A workshop by Connie Griffith at Indian Run Church, Dublin, Ohio. It stated in part:"Every form of spiritual discipline is a pathway by which we draw nearer to the Divine Light. It is advertised as follows:
"Place: Indian Run Church, at the corner of Avery and Brand Roads in Dublin, Ohio. ..."; "This event is sponsored by Epiphanies, Inc...."
- From a descriptive flier on the event itself
[Paul E. Miller was listed as pastor of Indian Run UMC in Dublin.]

October 13, 1996. "Food for the Soul" - The event was described as: "An afternoon to whet the spiritual appetite at Indian Run Church, Dublin, Ohio.....Leader: Paul E. Miller is the pastor of Indian Run United Methodist Church in Dublin and president of Epiphanies,Inc..." Workshops included, among others:
At the Side of the Well: Buddhism and Christianity.'" ...we will explore the common threads that exist between Christianity and Buddhism, with a special emphasis on the basic teachings of the

Buddha. Leader: Susan Richie,...minister of the Dublin Unitarian Universalist Church,...simply can't stop telling Buddhist parables."

"Eastern Spiritual Healing Coming West."...Chi Lei Qigong is a 5000-year old Chinese healing practice. It uses life-force energy to enhance the body's natural healing capacity....This event is sponsored by Epiphanies, Inc.   - From a flier on the event itself.

November, 1996. The Fourth Re-Imagining Conference. The two-day conference was titled "Naming, Claiming and ReImagining Power." Participants gathered under the themes of "Embodied Spirituality" (celebrating the power of women's sexuality),...and "Ecclesial Subversion" (brainstorming ways to overturn a "patriarchal" Church).

From an attendee, we have: "I (i.e., The Rev. Donna Hailson) took my place at one of the nearly 70 round tables. The 'talking circle' around each table was supposed to provide a 'safe space,' where all had equal voice and any question could be asked. At the first opening, I identified myself as an evangelical woman who had come in an attempt to understand the Re-Imagining Community. A woman, seated to my left, leapt up from the table and alerted the leadership to my presence. Two conference coordinators came to the table and asked the women what they wanted to do with me...Ironically, this occurred during the segment on 'Welcomed Differences.' I pointed out to these women that they were doing to me what they claim the Church has been doing to women for 2000 years: shutting me out....[There were also] the "Goddess Wall," at which nearly 40 goddesses were depicted with details on how each has been worshiped....the reinterpretation of the Fall which celebrates the "freedom and wisdom" that...Eve gained as she bit the apple....the use of the biblical term 'Sophia' (Wisdom) as a non-'gender-specific' substitute for Jesus....a 'paneroticism' that directly violates...sex only within faithful, heterosexual marriage."
- "No 'Safe Space' at Re-Imagining," by The Rev. Donna Hailson, FAITH & FREEDOM, Spring, 1997; p. 15.

December 6, 1997. "A Course in Miracles" - The article quotes Deb Rummel as saying, "The main premise of the course is that there are only two issues in the world, fear and love. As you move forward you realize fear is an illusion...." Also, "One of the key things for me is that there are thousands of ways to God. A Course in Miracles is only one of them." The last paragraph states, "The...group meets every Friday night at 7:30 p.m. in the United Methodist Church parlor..." [A more complete description is contained in the Timeline entry for May 24, 1998.]   - Lawrence County Centennial (Spearfish ed.); P. O. Box 797, Spearfish, South Dakota. Dec. 6, 1997; pp. 1, 2.

April, 1998. The "1998 Re-Imagining Revival" was held in Minneapolis, Minnesota. Approximately 170 United Methodists attended the event. Enshrouded in darkness, the "Re-Imagining community" gathered...on opening night to the throbbing of conference drummers. Overhead, lights flashed from a rotating, mirrored sphere while flames leaped from a four-foot cauldron on stage. "We are the light of the world," announced Rita Nakashima Brock.

"What does it take for us to break rank with the slave masters' religion?" asked another speaker, Carter Heyward. She proclaimed... that no person can claim to be unique, not even Jesus: "While nobody, even Jesus, is divine in and of him or herself, every body, like Jesus, is able to god, and I use this [god] as a verb...That is what we are to do...to god, and that is what the Jesus story is all about."

As Brock and others appeared on stage to deliver their speeches, ritual leaders carrying lanterns escorted them while the audience sang, "You are a lamp unto our feet and a light unto our path." then the crowd blessed each speaker, singing: "Now Sophia, dream the vision, share the wisdom dwelling deep within."

At a special denominational caucus at the event, United Methodists issued a statement commending and supporting those who have publicly stated their support for same-sex wedding ceremonies. "We understand these acts to be a faithful witness, calling the UMC to invite 'all persons to be full participants in the life of the church, both in policy and practice.'... Jeanne Audrey Powers, a retired UM ecumenical executive from Minneapolis...issued the statement on behalf of the Women's Caucus. - Good News, July/August 1998, pp. 34-36.

May 24, 1998. A Course in Miracles: Section B of "Life & Style"(p.1b)...The depiction on the front shows a multicolored cloud with the faces of Jesus Christ, (what appears to be) Buddha, the Star of David, a crescent moon, and two closed eyes. Groups also meet in Hot Springs, Spearfish and other outlying towns.... The article goes on to say: "When a co-worker and friend offered Boernke a copy of the three-volume book back in 1986, she didn't know she'd just been given a book of sacred Scripture....that reveals the highest spiritual truths, much as the Bible, the Koran, the Talmud, the I Ching or the Bhagavad-Gita do for the followers of the world's great religions. Like those great books, 'A Course in Miracles' is a book you never really finish. But unlike those other spiritual writings, it is modern-day scripture...." For many of its students, the course becomes their sole spiritual path, replacing organized religion in their life....[Nano] Johnson, whose Catholic faith was replaced by 'A Course in Miracles' [stated] 'It gives me God in my life.'
- The Rapid City Journal, May 24, 1998, Rapid City, South Dakota.

October 18, 1998. A program bulletin from "United Methodist Church" in Spearfish, South Dakota, dated October 18, 1998, shows that "Course on Miracles" meets in the parlor of the church at 7:00 P.M. on Wednesdays; "Mysticism of Now: the Art of Being Alive" meets in the parlor at 7:30 on Thursdays.
- Bulletin from "United Methodist Church" in Spearfish, South Dakota, dated October 18, 1998.

November 5, 1998. Eighth Annual Feminist Spirituality Annual Retreat, held at the Storm Mountain Retreat Center (located 11 1/2 miles south of Rapid City). The front of the flyer reads in part, "Deepening into our wholeness. Sponsored by COSROW - Dakota Conference of the UMC,..." Under the heading "Deepening into our wholeness" we find, "We will spend the weekend weaving a deep containing silence in which to share our deepest experience as women, naming into the silence our hopes, our pain, our fears. It is suggested that you read Judith (Duerk's} books, "Circle of Stones; Woman's Journey to Herself," and "I sit Listening to the Wind..."   - Brochure advertising the event.

Spring, 1999. The spring meeting of the Women's Division of the GBGM showcased attitudes of postmodern thought in several areas:

The Report of the Deputy General Secretary, Joyce SohI,...stated that, "Definitions of spirituality were as numerous as the writers and depend on the religious perspective whether Jewish, Christian, Buddhist or even New Age."...One handout at the director's meeting was Sing Out New Visions... Prayers, Poems and Reflections by Women....One prayer begins, "Breath of Life, Holy Spirit, Our Creator, Redeemer and Sustainer, You are the God called by many names: El, Yahweh, Adonai, Grandfather Spirit, Allah, Buddha, Ruach...." Several prayers and litanies are addressed to the goddess Sophia.
- Letter from Mrs. Faye Short, RENEW network, P. O. Box 889, Cornelia, Georgia 30531; dated July 1999.

May/June, 1999. Enforcing inclusive language. [Note: This is included since past experience has shown that the issues and problems we face in the UMC parallel those faced in the Presbyterian Church (USA) {PCUSA} and other mainline denominations, but especially those in the PCUSA. The "Overtures" mentioned here compare with petitions sent to our quadrennial general conference; their *Book of Order* compares to our *Book of Discipline*.] "Overture 99-24 from the Western New York Presbytery would amend the *Book of Order* to read, 'In its worship the church shall use language about God which is intentionally as diverse and varied as the Bible and our theological traditions.'...If Overture 99-24 is adopted, it would make it possible for charges to be filed against a minister who baptized 'in the name of the Father, Son and Holy

Spirit.' Similarly, an elder leading worship who began the Lord's Prayer 'Our Father' would be liable to disciplinary action.
- "Enforcing inclusive God-language" - an analysis, by Robert P. Mills; *The Presbyterian Layman*, May/June 1999; pages 1, 18.

Appendix E

Historical Homosexual Highlights

In order to determine where a person or institution is headed, it is helpful to review the past. In light of the recent outcomes of same-sex ceremonies performed by UM pastors, we need to take a look at different homosexual milestones affecting our denomination:

1972 General Conference. The following statement was added to the "Social Principles" document (after a 4 year study of homosexuality): "Homosexuals no less than heterosexuals are persons of sacred worth, who need the ministry and guidance of the church in their struggles for human fulfillment, as well as the spiritual and emotional care.... Further we insist that all persons are entitled to have their human and civil rights ensured, although we do not condone the practice of homosexuality and consider this practice incompatible with Christian teaching." In 1992, it was passed again with a vote of 75% in favor.

- United Methodist News Service (UMNS)

1976 General Conference. Adopted reports which stopped any funding of gay/lesbian support groups with church money. *- UMNS*

1980 General Conference. No significant action passed.*- UMNS*

1981. Affirmation (United Methodists for Gay and lesbian Concerns) protested the recent removal of gay and lesbian ministers from the pulpit and charged the UM Church with witch-hunting.

- Good News

1982. * Bishop Melvin E. Wheatley appointed Julian Rush, a self-avowed homosexual, as associate pastor of St. Paul's UM Church in Denver. Charges that Wheatley's stance had undermined "the authority of Holy Scripture" were filed by three Georgia churches.

An investigative committee said in its final report that it found no "reasonable grounds" for accusing the bishop. - *Good News*

* Phyllis Jean Athey and Mary Jo Osterman were united in a covenanting service at the Wheadon UMC in the Northern Illinois Conference.

1983 - 1984. * Roy Howard Beck of the United Methodist Reporter wrote on homosexual activities discovered at the general board level, including that by a bishop. He was told by Rev. Troy D. Perry, founder of the Fellowship of Metropolitan Community Churches, that a substantial percentage of mainline Protestant agency leaders were homosexual"...and allusions to sexual (both hetero- and homo-) misconduct by the clergy and members of the national boards and agencies. This was subsequently described in his book On Thin Ice.

* Phyllis Jean Athey and Mary Jo Osterman co-authored The Lesbian Relationship Handbook, published by Kinheart, an organization partially funded by the Northern Illinois Conference.

* A 3,500-member church in Colorado Springs "publicly censured" its bishop, Melvin E. Wheatley, for his active support of homosexual persons as UM ministers.
- *Good News*

1984 General Conference. Passed a "fidelity in marriage and celibacy in singleness" statement.
- *UMNS*

1986. The Rocky Mountain Annual Conference's Board of Ordained Ministry voted to dismiss the Julian Rush case.
- *Good News*

1987. UM Bishop Finis Crutchfield died at age 70 of AIDS.
- *Good News*

1988. * Phyllis Jean Athey, candidate for deacon in the UMC, shot and killed herself. Bishop J. R. Dewitt was critical of those who opposed her ordination on Biblical grounds for "causing this tragic act"; investigation pointed to the breakup with her lesbian "partner" Mary Jo Osterman.

* Opposition was surfaced to the partial funding, by the Northern Illinois Conference, of Kinheart Women's Center in Evanston, Illinois, believed to be a center for advocacy of homosexuality.

* General Conference. Voted to prohibit ordination of homosexuals by a vote of 676 to 293, or 69.76%. Yet, a measure was pushed through allocating $200,000 for a "Committee to Study Homosexuality," weighted with those supportive of the homosexual lifestyle. The General Council on Ministries (GCOM) conducted "An Analysis of Major Issues Addressed by the 1988 General Conference and a Comparison with Beliefs and Attitudes of Local Church Members." 765 out of 941 (or 81.296%) of those delegates surveyed agreed with the statement that "homosexuality is incompatible with Christian teaching." - *Good News*, Nov.-Dec. 1990

* **June 6, 1988.** Date of a letter sent out by Jimmy Creech, chairperson, of the Raleigh Religious Network for Gay and Lesbian Equality (RRNGLE), and UM pastor of Fairmount United Methodist Church in Raleigh, NC, that delineated the priorities espoused by RRNGLE: repeal the Crimes Against Nature Law (CAN); legalize and recognize lesbian and gay relationships; preserve parental and adoptive rights of lesbians and gays; etc.

1989. * Correspondence on the letterhead of Bishop C. P. Minnick, Jr., of the North Carolina Conference and dated January 18, 1989 was sent to pastors encouraging attendance at a two day conference sponsored by the Raleigh Religious Network for Gay and Lesbian Equality (RRNGLE).

* The United Methodist Committee to Study Homosexuality met for the first time to begin its four-year study. -

- *Good News*

* **Summer, 1989.** The following was published in the Summer, 1989 edition of The Christian Methodist Newsletter:

"Why is so much time and attention given to the term 'homophobia'? Is it to make it a topic of discussion so that the practice of homosexuality will ever so gradually be made acceptable to us by making its practitioners appear as victims?"

1990. Theologian Richard John Neuhaus reported on a pro-homosexual campaign to change church teaching through the premise that Christian doctrine and morality are "fundamentally in error." The UM Commission on Christian unity and Interreligious Concerns voted to include homosexuals. Dumbarton UMC of Washington, DC, decided against allowing a lesbian couple to wed after bowing to intense pressure.

1991. The Homosexuality Study Task Force completed three years' work on August 25 and announced it was unable to reach "a common mind" on whether the practice of homosexuality is compatible with Christian faith. "UM theologian Thomas Oden. of Drew University in New Jersey, was critical of the final report. Telling Christianity Today that the denomination's commitment to the primacy of Scripture is "blatantly falsified and misrepresented in the report's appeal to experience and reason as contemporary arbiters of the hidden meaning of Scripture. "The committee has asked GCOM to recommend a church-wide study of homosexuality with the denomination developing study materials to be used by individuals, congregations, and annual conferences."

-Adapted from UMNS, as reported in Good News Magazine

1992. * A letter signed by 100 clergy and laity in Michigan supported homosexual and lesbian "holy union" services.

* Saralyn Chesnut has been named to head the new office of Lesbian, Gay, and Bisexual Student Life at (UM) Emory University.

* UM Bishop Melvin G. Talbert, joined others in calling on President-elect Bill Clinton to lift the military ban on homosexuals.

* **General Conference 1992**. Rejected both the majority report of the "Committee to Study Homosexuality" and the accompanying "augmentation Paragraph" of the "Social Principles" affirming "same-sex relationships"; a minority report of the "Committee to Study Homosexuality" reaffirmed the traditional church position.

- UMNS

On Monday, May 11, after an afternoon of debate, demonstration and testimony, the 1992 General Conference, by a 710-238 vote, reaffirmed its 20-year stand that the practice of homosexuality is "incompatible with Christian teaching." In retaining the...Social Principles statement, delegates were also rejecting the controversial recommendation of the four-year homosexuality study report which asked that the phrase he deleted because of the church's "lack of a common mind." In a separate vote. delegates did receive, by a 767 to 190 margin, the amended report of the Homosexuality Study Task Force, asking General Conference to "make it [the report] available for study and use across the whole church." A second recommendation said, "We recommend the development of resources consistent with the Social Principles of the United Methodist Church which support ministry to and with homosexual persons.

A strategic point in the floor debate came when the Rev. Kasongo Munza, delegate from Zaire, addressed the conference through an interpreter. The African pastor, in an impassioned voice, called the practice of homosexuality "unbiblical and non-Christian," and said any change in the church's stand would be "a source of terrible division and could destroy the church of our Lord." He added, "We don't want our culture contaminated by what we consider to be a disease."

At a news conference following the vote, the Rev. Tex Sample, professor at St. Paul School of Theology in Kansas City. and a supporter of removing the "incompatible" phrase, said, "It's going to take 10 years, or 20 years, or 25 years, but this church will change its position. The victory is coming. The Rev. David Seamands, professor at Asbury Theological Seminary in Wilmore, Kentucky, and a strong supporter of the church's present language, said that to change the statement "would have sent a signal that we condone homosexuality because it is compatible with scripture." - *Good News*

1993. * Pentecost, 1993. Letter to the North Carolina Christian Advocate Concerning Annual Conference Action Taken Regarding the North Carolina Council of Churches by The Reverend Ben Sharpe, Jr. explained the doctrinal basis of incompatibility of the Universal Fellowship of Metropolitan Community Churches with true Christianity.

* June, 1993. The North Carolina Annual Conference. By a vote of the delegation, all funding to the North Carolina Council of Churches (NCCC) was discontinued because of the NCCC's admission into its membership the Universal Fellowship of the Metropolitan Community Churches (MCC), which accepts the practice of homosexuality as an alternative Christian lifestyle. A last-minute effort by supporters of the NCCC was narrowly defeated.
- Allen O. Morris, observer.

* In November, the "Re-Imagining" Conference was conducted which affirmed lesbians, bisexuals, and "trans-gendered" people, and which was supported in part by UM money.

1993 - 1994. Members of Concerned Methodists were told that, over the space of the year between the two annual conferences, Bishop C.P. Minnick, Jr. had stressed at two cabinet meetings that he wanted the funding restored to the North Carolina Council of Churches.

1994. * February, 1994. A "listening session" was held on the issue of restoring funding to the NCCC by the The North Carolina Conference.

* June, 1994. The North Carolina Annual Conference. Bishop C.P. Minnick, Jr. asked that the funding be restored to the NCCC with the thought that "a message had been sent" to the NCCC. The discontinuance of all funding to the North Carolina Council of Churches (NCCC) from the conference was maintained by a vote of approximately 78% of the delegates because the NCCC had maintained its relationship with the MCC.

1996. * 1996 General Conference. Voted 577 - 378 (60.4%) to approve the church's current stance in paragraph 71F that homosexuality is incompatible with Christian teaching" and 553 - 321 to add to the Book of Discipline's "Social Principles" a statement prohibiting ceremonies that celebrate homosexual unions.

* April 18, 1996. Fifteen bishops express "pain" over church policy on gay, lesbian issues.
DENVER (UMNS) — Fifteen United Methodist bishops — 11 active, four retired — released a statement here April 18 expressing "pain ... over our personal convictions that are contradicted by the proscriptions in the (Book of Discipline against gay and lesbians within our church and within our ordained and diaconal ministers." - News release by UMNS at the 1996 General Conference of the UMC, Denver, Colorado. (A copy of the original release is contained in Appendix G)

1997. * September 14. Jimmy Creech conducted a service of union for two women, who attended FUMC in Omaha, Nebraska, which he pastored.

- UMNS

* In 1997, Emory's board of trustees, which includes five United Methodist bishops [to include Lindsey Davis of the North Georgia Conference], voted unanimously to allow same-sex ceremonies in the university chapel...if the ceremony is conducted by a clergy person of that faith who has a tie to the university. [Bishop Solomon was on travel.]

- Alice Smith, Executive Director of the Georgia UM Communications Council.

1998. * March 13, 1998. Thirty UM clergy have publicly declared that they will "celebrate rites of union with all couples, regardless of gender...." The "Proclaiming the Vision Committee" invited UM clergy to sign such a statement. - From the INTERNET and Newscope, March 13, 1998.

* March, 1998. Kearney, Nebraska: ...Jimmy Creech, pastor of FUMC in Omaha, was acquitted of wrongdoing in his performance of a "covenanting ceremony" between two women alleged to be lesbians. - *The Fayetteville Observer-Times, March 14, 1998*

* March 17, 1998. In a letter to the bishops dated March 17th, Dr. Maxie Dunmam, president of Asbury Theological Seminary, wrote, "If the practice of same-sex marriages is allowed to stand...our beloved denomination will be seriously fractured if not completely divided... if we have to call a special session of the General Conference to prevent such schismatic action, let's do so. My heart is heavy. I am grieving for the church."

* March 17, 1998. UNITED METHODISTS DENOUNCE CREECH VERDICT
An ad hoc group of pastors and lay persons from The United Methodist Church denounced the verdict in a church trial last week which acquitted a minister charged with violating church law. The Reverend Jimmy Creech of First United Methodist Church in Omaha, Nebraska had performed a "same sex covenant service" for two lesbian women last September...and [was] acquitted of the charge when only eight of the thirteen jurors in the case found him in violation of the Church's ban on performing homosexual marriages. Included among the signatories of the statement are Bob and Betty Howell and Diane West, members of First United Methodist Church in Omaha.
[List of signatories omitted due to length.]

* April, 1998. Letter from Hankyu Park, superintendent of the Shasta District of the California-Nevada Conference, said in part: ",...but supported Bethany United Methodist Church when they made decision to allow a ceremony for same sex unions to be held in their facility."

* July 22, 1998. E-mail from Bob Kuyper, Editor, Transforming Congregations, who references an article from World Magazine.

Two very interesting quotes in the article are 1) about Bishop Talbert and why he has not appointed an evangelical to be a District Superintendent: "For ERF [i.e., "Evangelical Renewal Fellowship"] members, it's not just doctrinal differences that have disheartened them. They complain that not one evangelical has been appointed to a conference leadership position. Asked about this seeming lack of commitment to tolerance and diversity, Bishop Talbert told WORLD: 'Look, I need to appoint people whom I can trust implicitly, because they represent me.'"So much for inclusion...

- E-mail; Bob Kuyper, July 22, 1998.
http://www.worldmag.com/world/home.asp

* August,1998. The statement (proscribing same-sex ceremonies) is contained in the Social Principles section of the Book of Discipline, whereas the rest of the denomination's binding rules are contained in the main section of the book. However, the United Methodist Judicial Council, the denomination's supreme court, ruled...that the statement is enforceable.

- by UMNS; (10-21-28{291}

1999: * January 16, 1999. 69 United Methodist pastors of the California-Nevada Annual Conference co-officiated in a "holy union" service for two women Ellie Charlton and Jeanne Barnett, two members of Sacramento St. Mark's United Methodist Church, where the Rev. Donald Fado is pastor. Ellie is a member of the Conference Board of Trustees. Jeanne is conference lay leader.

List of persons accused of participating: John J. Auer, III, Brandon Austin, Donald L. Baldwin, Claire Beals-Nesmith, Robert W. Blaney, Diana Marie Bohn, Richard E. Bruner, Carol M. Carter,

George Carter, Jerry Carter, John Chamberlin, Thomas Clark, Rolfe Conrad, Clifford Crummey, Donna Morrow DeCamp, Sharon Delgado, Nadine DeWitt, Steven Eatough-Smith, Janet S. Everhart, Renae Extrum-Fernandez, Donald Fado, David Franks, Glenn Fuller, Nobuaki Hanaoka, J. Richard Hart, Robert J. Hawthorne, Douglas Hayward, Thomas Hicks, Bruce Hilton, Virginia Hilton, Elbert Hoffman, Hubert L. Ivery, Alan H. Jones, Linda Kelly, Phillip Lawson, Stephen Lee, Charles Lerrigo, James Lockwood-Stewart, David MacMurdo, Theresa Mason, Victor W. McLane, Maggie McNaught, Douglas Monroe, Bob Moon, Mike Morizono, Mary Parker-Eves, Larry Patten, Ted Pecot, Cheri Pierre, Jay Pierce, Kathleen Ralston, Robert Rankin, Lynn Rhodes, Byron Roberts, Ellen Rowan, Robert Sanford, Doug Smith, Marlene Spilman, Judith Stone, Frank H. Stone, Gerald Summers, Paul Sweet, Margo Tenold, Harold A. Tillinghast, Richard Whitmore, Cecil Williams, Lee Williamson, Andrea Meek Winchester, Sargent Wright.

- UMNS #157; Nashville,Tennessee 10-21-28-71BP{157}

* January 21, 1999. The Reverend Mike Goodyear lodged a complaint against Don Fado, pastor of St. Mark's United Methodist Church, who co-officiated in a holy "union service" for two women, Ellie Charlton and Jeanne Barnett, in Sacramento.

- E-mail received at Concerned Methodists, Inc.

* March 4, 1999. Union In Northern California. Members of a Sacramento area church filed 184 formal complaints against 92 Methodist ministers who performed a controversial "holy union"ceremony for a lesbian couple...The complaints lodged by the Reverend Mike Goodyear [on January 21st] and members of FUMC in Orangevale, California stem from the highly publicized January ceremony where 92 dissident ministers blessed the relationship of Jeanne Barnett and Ellie Charlton.
- Don Lattin, Religion Writer, San Francisco Chronicle, March 4, 1999

* March 4-7, 1999. WASHINGTON (UMNS) - The United Methodist Board of Church and Society [GBCS] approved proposals to change two paragraphs on human sexuality....at the General Conference in Cleveland, May 2-12, 2000....Bishop Melvin Talbert, as chairman of the board's human welfare work area, presented the committee's recommendation [to]: "We affirm that God's grace is available to all."

- UMNS; March 10, 1999; Washington 10-71BP{129}

* **March 23, 1999.** Bishop Talbert announced complaint against 69 pastors.   - Multiple news sources

* **March 26, 1999.** Dell convicted in same-sex ceremony. Following the ruling [by the United Methodist Judicial Council], the Rev. Greg Dell of Chicago performed a (same-sex) ceremony and was found guilty in a church trial. (Bishop Joe) Sprague, who filed the charge, said he had hoped to frame it in a way to provide a "teachable moment" for the church. While he believes that occurred, he added that the trial also has shown the world "the box we have put ourselves into in this denomination"....the pastor had performed the Sept. 19 union ceremony between Keith Eccarius and Karl Reinhardt at Broadway United Methodist Church. Along with disregarding the authority of the United Methodist General Conference, the denomination's highest legislative body, Dell ignored the decision of its highest court, the church counsel said.... He has conducted 33 such ceremonies in the past 18 years.

- UMNS#168, March 29, 1999; New York; 10-21-71BP{168}

[The following commentary was offered by a pastor who had observed the proceedings: "The counsel for the church, allowed without objection, three homosexuals to share the validity of their lifestyle. One came from a reformed church where theology was done by using "scripture, scripture, scripture, and scripture." The other was the son of a Missouri Synod pastor who has come to accept his son's lifestyle. All of this presentation of a testimony of the validity of the homosexual lifestyle was presented without objection by the counsel of the church.]

- E-mail dated Sun, 28 Mar 1999

* April, 1999. A complaint has been filed against Reverend Mike Goodyear by his district superintendent, David Bennett. Goodyear is the pastor of the Orangevale Church, whose parishioners had filed charges against Pastor Don Fado other members of the California-Nevada Conference for participating in a "same-sex" covenanting ceremony. While the charges Goodyear and his congregation filed against Greg Dell and the participants in the "same sex" ceremony had been stalled by the judicial process in the conference, those against Goodyear have been put on the "fast track" for prosecution.

- E-mail from UM pastor

* In other action, the evangelical people of St. Francis UMC in the Golden Gate District of that conference face closure of their church (see case study in Appendix Q). Projection now is that St. Francis, with a multiracial Philippino and Anglo congregation, will cease to exist.
- From Personal Assistance provided to St. Francis by Concerned Methodists

* April 10, 1999. Announcement was made of the transfer of Dr. Charles Sineath of FUMC Marietta comes nearly a year after the church voted to withhold $58,427 in funds from the local conference over the national church's stands on social issues, including homosexuality.
- Source: E-mail; *The Atlanta Journal-Constitution; By Tucker McQueen.*

* April 14, 1999. Creech, on leave of absence from active ministry in the Nebraska Conference, performed a ceremony for two men at a church in Chapel Hill, N.C., on April 24.

* April 15, 1999. Georgia church withholds funds amid talk of split. ATLANTA (UMNS) — The board of stewards of Marietta First United Methodist Church has voted to withhold all of the financial support that it typically provides at the conference and denominational levels. The church's total apportionments for 1999

are $268,087. Previously the church had decided to withhold about $67,000 of that amount.
- Internet, April 15, 1999; Nashville, TN. 10-21-71{203; by Alice Smith, Ex. Dir. of the Georgia UM Communications Council

* April 27, 1999. As of 1 A. M. EDT today, Charles (Sineath) has been relieved of all responsibilities, by Mr. Davis [i.e., Bishop Davis], as pastor of FUMC-Marietta. The reason for this action is that he is to be named tonight as the new pastor of a new church in Marietta.
- Source: Internet, E-mail from B.J. Eble, former member of FUMC Marietta, Georgia; April 27, 1999 12:31 PM

* May 12, 1999. SMU board adds sexual orientation to policy.
- Information adapted from a May 7 news release from the News and Information Office of Southern Methodist University; *UMNS #269*

* May 25, 1999. Complaints filed against Creech over same-sex union ceremony. The complaints were filed with the Bishop Joel Martinez, head of the United Methodist Church's Nebraska Annual (regional) Conference. Creech, on leave of absence from active ministry in the Nebraska Conference, performed the ceremony for two men at a church in Chapel Hill, N.C., on April 24.
- By UMNS; (10-21-28-71BP{291}

* May 27, 1999. Methodists Accept Report on Gays. Oklahoma United Methodists voted narrowly to accept a task force report on ministries relating to homosexuality after amending the report to soften... language. "Have we gotten used to the smell of sin?" asked the Rev. Clarence R. Shahan, the pastor in Hitchcock. "We all sin. But we don't promote sin. This is the word of God, from Genesis to Revelation. Let us accept one another, but let us not promote sin."
- The Oklahoman; 5/27/1999; By Pat Gilliland, Religion Editor

* May 27, 1999. Layman files complaint against Denver bishop. A complaint filed against United Methodist Bishop Mary Ann

Swenson of Denver will be reviewed by her peers in the denomination's Western Jurisdiction. Mel Brown, a layman from Johnstown, Colorado, made two charges against Swenson in a letter to Bishop Ed Paup of Portland, Ore., president of the Western Jurisdiction College of Bishops. Brown said he had complained to Swenson on August 28 that the Rev. Toni Cook, pastor of St. Paul's United Methodist Church in Denver, "has been conducting same-sex marriages for some time" but that he had received no response from Swenson about his complaint.

- By Personal Interview; *UMNS: (10-21-28-71B{301}*

* June 10, 1999. The Rev. Greg Dell, convicted in a March church trial for performing a same-sex union, has been elected as a delegate to the United Methodist Church's top legislative body, along with the pastor who defended him.

- *UMNS; June 10, 1999;* Nashville, Tenn. 10-21-28-71BP{324)

* June 15, 1999. Reaction to the recent decision by the United Methodist Women's division to support a homosexual and lesbian alliance has left many in the denomination confused or angry. The largest church women's organization in America is financially supporting a homosexual student group's quest to gain official acceptance at a Salt Lake City high school. The group, called the Gay/ Straight Alliance, currently rents space at East High, but the group is waging a war to gain free space at the school. Mark Tooley of the Institute on Religion (IRD) and Democracy says the leaders of the UMW are ignoring the teachings of the church by lending support - ...$11,000. [Note: Mr. Mark Tooley is a member of UMAction]

- American Family Radio News; June 15, 1999; http://www.afr.net

Additional information: At its spring meeting, the Women's Division directors voted approval for a grant of $11,000 to "Free School Clubs." A few directors questioned whether or not this grant could be considered as promoting homosexuality among high school students.... The information compiled indicates that the $11,000 grant will help fund meetings that will rally support behind the

Gay/Straight Alliance [which]...has gleaned support for its legal campaign from the New York Gay, Lesbian and Straight Education Network (GLSEN), the American Civil Liberties Union and the Lambda Legal Defense Fund - Letter from Mrs. Faye Short, *RENEW network; dated July 1999*

* June 18, 1999. 'Sacramento 68' investigation will likely be long. The committee in charge of investigating a complaint against 68 California-Nevada United Methodist ministers has scheduled meetings into September, but the process will likely go beyond then, according to the panel's chairman. "This will probably be a long process, as we see it," said the Rev. Ron Swisher, head of the committee on investigation...Bishop Melvin G. Talbert, head of the United Methodist Church's California-Nevada Annual (regional) Conference, announced in March that the complaint had been filed against the clergy members. At the same time, Talbert reiterated his own opposition to the church's strictures against same-sex services.
- UMNS #338; June 18, 1999; Nashville, Tenn.; 10-21-28-71B{338}

* June 30, 1999. The United Methodist Board of Church and Society has again thrown its support behind a bill that would grant all persons, regardless of sexual orientation, federal protection from workplace discrimination. An Employment Non-discrimination Act (ENDA) was supported by the board when it was first introduced in 1997...Urging the Congress to pass a new Employment Non-discrimination Act introduced last week, Fassett said..., "It would extend to homosexuals the same civil rights protections in the workplace as are accorded women, minorities, people with disabilities and religious persons."
- UMNS #360; June 30, 1999; Nashville, Tenn.; 10-21-28-71B{360}

* July 8, 1999. Rev. Gregory Dell's Broadway United Methodist Church in Chicago...is allowing Dell and his wife Jade to continue living in its parsonage and has created a new year-long, three-quarter time position for him as executive director of "In All Things Char-

ity," the first paid position for that...group which advocates within the denomination for...gays and lesbians.
- *The Chicago News Planet, July 8, 1999.*

* August 2, 1999. "Young people struggle with homosexuality issue" KNOXVILLE, Tenn. (UMNS) - Young people in the United Methodist Church, like the adults, are not of one mind on the thorny topic of homosexuality. Issues related to homosexuality were a focus of workshops held during Youth '99, the five-day gathering sponsored by the United Methodist Board of Discipleship. The 9,000 teens at the event each had a choice of attending four out of about 500 workshops. One young person questioned whether homosexuality is a matter of choice or genetics. "If it is genetic, why would God create something against the Bible?" the youth asked. "I don't think gay people should be ordained," the teen continued. "Pastors are supposed to be Christian and like God. Being gay is a sin...." "I think you are born gay," another participant replied...."It (the Bible) was translated from another language. How do we know it is right? The Bible was written so many years ago; times have changed."
- *UMNS #401, Aug. 2, 1999. Nashville, Tenn.; 10-28-71B{401}*

Appendix F

Letter from
Bishop C. P. Minnick, Jr.'s Office

The United Methodist Church
RALEIGH AREA
The Methodist Building, 1307 Glenwood Avenue
Post Office Box 10955
Raleigh, North Carolina 27605-0955

C.P. MINNICK, JR.
Resident Bishop

January 18, 1989

Office (919) 832-9560
Residence (919) 782-0520

TO: UNITED METHODIST PASTORS

FROM: BISHOP C. P. MINNICK, JR.

My dear Sisters and Brothers:

On March 10-11 the Raleigh Religious Network for Gay and Lesbian
Equality will sponsor a conference in Raleigh at Pullen Memorial
Baptist Church. This conference is designed to equip us as pastors to minister more effectively and more meaningfully to gay
men and lesbians and their families in our congregations and in
the larger community. The topic for this conference will be
"Homophobia in the Religious Community."

This letter is my endorsement of this event and my encouragement
to you to avail yourselves of this opportunity to enhance your
understanding of the fears, the hate and the hostility toward
homosexual persons and their families. These emotions are expressed in so many painful and destructive ways in our churches
and society. Homophobia is an urgent pastoral care issue which
we need to address. You will be receiving more data and information about this conference from the Network in the near future.

May God continue to bless and use you as you seek to be in a
ministry of caring concern to all persons in the name and spirit
of Jesus Christ.

CPMJr/vm

113

Appendix G

News Release by the "Denver 15"

United Methodist
General Conference

1996 General Conference

In Essentials Unity
In Non-Essentials Liberty
In All Things Charity

April 16-26

1996

Colorado Convention Center
Denver, Colorado
News Room: (303)446-4220

Newsroom coordinated by United Methodist News Service, a unit of United Methodist Communications

TITLE: Bishops Express Pain Over Gay Issue
SEARCH: homosexuality, gay, lesbian, ordination,

010 (2974)   April 18, 1996

General Conference '96

Fifteen bishops express 'pain' over
church policy on gay, lesbian issues

DENVER (UMNS) -- Fifteen United Methodist bishops -- 11
active, four retired -- released a statement here April 18
expressing "pain ... over our personal convictions that are
contradicted by the proscriptions in the (Book of) Discipline
against gay and lesbians within our church and within our ordained
and diaconal ministers."

Nevertheless, they affirmed their commitment to uphold the
Discipline of the church.

"We believe it is time to break the silence and state where
we are on this issue that is hurting and silencing countless
faithful Christians," the bishops say. "We will continue our
responsibility to the order and discipline of the church but urge
United Methodist churches to open the doors in gracious
hospitality to all brothers and sisters in the faith."

Portions of the Disciplinary paragraphs to which the bishops
refer say:
-- the church does not condone the practice of homosexuality
and considers the practice "incompatible with Christian teaching";
-- "self-avowed practicinng homosexuals are not to be
accepted as candidates, ordained as ministers, or appointed to
serve The United Methodist Church";
-- no churchwide money may be given to any "gay caucus or
group" or be used to "promote the acceptance of homosexuality."

The 11 active bishops signing the statement were: Judith
Craig, Ohio West Area; William W. Dew Jr., Portland (Ore.) Area;
Calvin D. McConnell, Seattle Area; Susan M. Morrison,
Philadelphia Area; Fritz Mutti, Kansas Area; Donald A. Ott,

-MORE-

Michigan Area; Sharon Zimmerman Rader, Wisconsin Area; Roy I.
Sano, Los Angeles Area; Mary Ann Swenson, Denver Area; Melvin G.
Talbert, San Francisco Area; and Joseph H. Yeakel, Washington
Area.

Retired bishops signing the statement were: C. Dale White,
Newport, R.I.; Jesse R. DeWitt, Naperville, Ill.; Leontine T.C.
Kelly, San Mateo, Calif.; and Melvin G. Wheatley Jr., Laguna
Hills, Calif.

.#

Full text of the bishops' statement:

We the undersigned bishops wish to affirm the commitment made
at our consecration to the vows to uphold the _Discipline_ of the
church. However, we must confess the pain we feel over our
personal convictions that are contradicted by the proscriptions in
the _Discipline_ against gay and lesbian persons within our church
and within our ordained and diaconal ministers. Those sections
are paragraphs 71F (last paragraph); 402.2; 906.12; and footnote
p. 205.

We believe it is time to break the silence and state where we
are on this issue that is hurting and silencing countless faithful
Christians. We will continue our responsibility to order and
discipline of the church but urge our United Methodist churches to
open the doors in gracioius hospitality to all our brothers and
sisters in the faith.

-- Tom McAnally

Appendix H

A Snapshot of the Gay Lifestyle

1. Scripture Talks about the Gay Lifestyle:

"...every passage which speaks of homosexual behaviors is clear, unambiguously negative and morally hostile towards them (the actions themselves)....Leviticus 18:22, 20:13, Romans 1:15-32, I Corinthians 6:9-10 and I Timothy 1:8-10 condemn them directly, while Genesis 19, Judges 19, I Peter 2:6-10, and Jude 7 do so indirectly.

- *"Blessing the Unblessable", by Professor David A. Seamands, Good News Magazine, November/December 1992.*

God's standard for the human race in terms of sexuality

- Genesis 1:27; 5:2: "male and female created he them"....It was God's plan for sexual relations to be in the form of man-woman union, man and wife becoming "one flesh" (Genesis 2:24).

- *"Is Homosexuality an Alternate Lifestyle?", by David Jeremiah, The Rebirth of America, The Arthur S. Demoss Foundation, 1986.*

- "Because man's sexual identity is defined by God, because his orientation is ordained by God, and because his sexual activity is circumscribed within a heterosexual marriage context, homosexuality cannot be viewed merely as a variant sexual preference or accidental variation within creation (akin to left-handedness)... Instead, it represents a choice, in some sense, to set one's desires and satisfy one's physical drives in a way contrary to God's appointment and creation. There is no natural homosexuality, for homosexuality is precisely a perversion of nature (understood as God's design for human relations). Homosexuals are made, not born; their disorder is developed contrary to their God-given identity, learned in opposition to the created order."

- *Homosexuality - A Biblical View, Greg L. Bahnsen.*

2. Rewards of the Gay Life:

Source of the plague of AIDS in the United States; average life expectancy is 41; with AIDS factored in, age is 39.1 (1); a study of 15,565 gay men has determined that, independent of HIV infection, homosexual men are 24 times more apt to get anal cancer than men in the general population (2). 43 percent of homosexuals have had over 500 encounters; 28 percent have had over 1000 (3). With the threat of AIDS, sexual contacts average 47 per year, 76 during pre-AIDS years (4); six times more likely to attempt suicide (5); 35 percent are alcoholics (6); 78 percent have been infected by some form of STD (7); 67 percent of all AIDS cases are directly attributable to homosexual conduct, and 50 percent of male homosexuals in San Francisco are now infected with the HIV virus that causes AIDS - up from 7 percent in the early 1980s (8).

3. Biblical Compassion for Gays:

"Like Christ, we must have compassion on the sinner while at the same time we are condemning the sin... Dr. Melvin Anchell said that whoever decided to call homosexuals "gay" must have had a terrible sense of humor. They are lonely, guilty, often depressed people. Their only hope is Jesus Christ, and we must be His caring ambassadors to them... The hope of the homosexual today is the same as it was in Paul's day. Jesus Christ can and will wash away any sin. The sin of homosexuality is not a stain too deep to respond to the cleansing power of his blood." - *Jeremiah, Rebirth.*

Observation #1: There are now more ex-homosexuals than there are active homosexuals (9).

Observation #2: The average age of the first homosexual experience is age 13 (Dr. Paul Cameron, The Family Research Institute)

Observation #3: There is no credible study that shows homosexuals are born with an innate predisposition toward that lifestyle.

Observation #4: Even if there were a credible study that shows homosexuals are born with a predisposition toward homosexuality (which there, assuredly, is not), that still does not justify behavior that is so deleterious to their health - just as if it were possible for someone to be born with a predisposition toward alcoholism, that does not mean that he has to drink and become an alcoholic.

Observation #5: Since the publication of Albert Kinsey's book *Sexual Behavior in the Human Male* had touted the figure of "10% of the male population being homosexual" there have been numerous studies discrediting that figure. A 1990 study of more than 10,000 persons by the National Center for Health Statistics indicates that homosexuals and bisexuals combined total approximately 1.5 percent (5, 10). Different studies we have seen at Concerned Methodists of varying male populations show the percentage to be between .8% and 2.4%.

Notes:
1. Dr. Paul Cameron of the Family Research Institute, P.O. Box 62640, Colorado Springs, Colorado 80962-2640.
2. Ibid., *Family Report*, January-February 1997, p. 2.
3. Kinsey study, as reported in *Homosexualities; A Study of Diversity among Men and Women*, by Alan P. Bell and Martin S. Weinberg, (New York, Simon and Schuster, 1978).
4. S.A. Seward, *USA Today*, November 21, 1984; L. McKusick, et. al., "AIDS and Sexual Behavior Reported by Gay Men in San Francisco," American Journal of Public Health, 1985, pp. 193-196.
5. Commander Eugene T. Gomulka, USMC, "Homosexuality in Uniform: Is It Time?", as reported in *Good News* Magazine, March/April 1993, p. 33. The original article appeared in the December 1992 *Proceedings of the U.S. naval Institute*. Commander Gomulka is a past Deputy Chaplain of the U.S. Marine Corps based in Washington, D.C.
6. Robert J. Kus, "Alcoholics Anonymous and Gay American Men," *Journal of Homosexuality*, Vol. 14, No. 2 (1987), p. 254.
7. American Public Health Association, as reported by Enrique T. Rueda, *The Homosexual Network* (Old Greenwich, Conn.: Devin Adair, 1982), p. 53.
8. Center for Disease Control, as reported by the Family Research Council, Robert G. Morrison, editor, "The Last Bastion," *Washington Watch*, June 1992, p. 1.

9. Dr. D. James Kennedy, "The Spiritual State of the Union," Coral Ridge Ministries, P. O. Box 40, Ft. Lauderdale, Florida 33340.

10. Deborah Dawson, "AIDS Knowledge and Attitudes for January-March 1990: Provisional Data from the National Health Interview Survey"; Joseph F. Fittle and Marcie Cynamon, ibid. for April-June 1990; Pamela F. Adams and Ann M. Hardy, ibid. for July-September 1990, in *Advance Data*, nos. 193, 195, and 198, National Center for Health Statistics, Centers for disease Control, Public Health Service, U. S. Department of Health and Human Services, p. 11 in all three documents.

* * * * * * *

I'm very scared to die such a young man. I'd like a little more time. I lived in the fast lane. If only God will give me a break."

- 28-year-old man infected with AIDS, TIME, August 12, 1985

Appendix I

Missionary Orientation
by The Reverend Max Borah

After a year and a half of correspondence with the GBGM, we were accepted as missionary candidates and asked to attend three weeks of missionary orientation. This was on very short notice— one week—but we jumped at the chance, feeling that after waiting so long in the application process we had better not seem hesitant now. Orientation took place July 6-29, 1983 at Stony Point Center, a beautiful Retreat Center about 60 miles north of New York City on the Hudson River.

There were 33 candidates going to several different countries: Ecuador, Uruguay, Argentina, Tonga, Zaire, Nigeria and Sierra Leone, among others. We represented a variety of occupations: ministers, teachers, doctors, nurses, airplane pilots, and maintenance. We were of different ages: from fresh out of college to retirement age. And, as we were soon to find out, we also represented very different theological perspectives. I was very interested in the fact that they were sending a missionary to Ecuador, since I had been told in some of our earliest correspondence with the Board that they "have no mission personnel there." We had inquired about service in Quito because I had been there with OMS on an Evangelism Crusade and found the potential for evangelism there almost unlimited.

As I came to know the head of the Latin American Office, I began to understand why Patty and I wouldn't have been considered for service in Ecuador. All, and I do mean all, the people going to South America are strong liberation theology people. The wife of a pastor going to Argentina told me that the reason they had been so attractive to the Latin American Office was because of the interest they had and belief they held in Liberation Theology, which she said was obvious in their application. It was this same group which literally booed President Reagan during a news conference that was broadcast during orientation.

Each morning began with what was called "Biblical Reflection". In fact, to me, it was neither Biblical nor reflective. Our Biblical Reflections speakers were quite liberal theologically. Two of them had been expelled from their homelands (Korea and Chile) for political involvement. These were the two who spoke more than any of the others. Dr. Han Wan Sang, an exile from South Korea, encouraged us not to be afraid to become politically involved in our host country. One of his Biblical Reflections studies was on the parable of the Good Samaritan. According to him this story shows us how people are enslaved by oppressive governments and multinational corporations. We, as missionaries, should be like the Good Samaritan and help free people from such oppression. He told us that "if you are expelled from your host country for political involvement, you will inherit eternal life." He openly admitted, "I am a Marxist."

The exile from Chile, Dr. Joel Gajardo, let us know in no uncertain terms that most, if not all, of the trouble in Latin America was due to the United States' foreign policy and multinational corporations. Marxism was praised, as was Nicaragua, Cuba, and the former Marxist government in Chile. He told us, "You cannot separate social action and evangelism because social action is evangelism."

Only twice do I recall our Biblical Reflections leaders having prayer with the group. We went through day after day together without seeking God's guidance for what we were doing.

One thing which came through clearly as Orientation continued was that the GBGM has no doctrine of sin. They simply ignore the influence and effects of sin in the world and speak instead of injustice. Injustice is sin to them. And it is that from which we, as missionaries, are to help deliver others.

It doesn't take long for one to realize that the theology currently in vogue in the Board is totally alien to that of Wesley and traditional Methodism. At best, the theology of the GBGM is a "mongrel", incorporating Universalism, a generous amount of Secular Humanism, and Liberation Theology. From what I could see, no Wesleyan Theology was present at all.

Our main subject of the day covered a variety of topics. We were introduced to many of the agencies, publications and personnel which are part of the GBGM. We found this both interesting and helpful. World Division staff personnel gave us an overview of the different areas of the world, including their respective priorities, goals, and perspectives for Latin America, Africa, Western Europe, China, and the Pacific Islands. Dr. Harry Haines gave a very challenging presentation to us.

We were informed about packing, income taxes, salary, pensions, health insurance, and the children's educational endowment, all of which I appreciated. To me, the most helpful speaker during Orientation was Dr. Duvon Corbitt, former missionary to Zaire. He spoke to us about potential health problems, ranging from dysentery to cerebral malaria to how to deliver a baby; and topics from how to light a gas refrigerator to how not to go crazy when you are dealing with a new language. Unfortunately, very little time was spent on such vital information. While only two hours were allotted Dr. Corbitt to discuss tropical diseases we would confront, two days were allotted to discuss the International Monetary Fund. (We all wondered just how that was going to help us in any significant way.)

On one occasion we were to hear a presentation on some of the other faiths we would confront. A former United Methodist missionary to Egypt spoke to us about Islam. We were very interested in this because there were many Muslims in our assigned country. His knowledge was vast and I enjoyed his presentation, but we were dismayed at the advice he gave us for dealing with them. "We shouldn't try to convert them," he said. "We should leave the converting to God." We should just "be friends" to them because "both Islam and Christianity reflect the glory of God." We were also told going to the field to convert the people to Christianity was a part of the 18th century, but thankfully we have outgrown that now.

One full day was given to a presentation by Catholic sisters from the Maryknoll Order. Their approach was openly anti-U.S., and very pro-Cuba, pro-Nicaragua. Part of their presentation involved dividing the group into different countries for a "Global Village Simulation Game." Each person was assigned to represent a different country: some rich - some poor - the world was divided along these lines. It was a big joke that no one wanted to be assigned to represent the United States because they were obviously the "bad guys".

We were told over and over in many different ways by many speakers that the United States' foreign policy was oppressive, as were multinational (usually American) corporations and capitalism in general. A redistribution of the world's wealth was proposed as a possible solution to the world's problems, along with a "new world order" built along Marxist lines. We were even asked during a meeting of our primary groups to discuss whether we would admit to being a U.S. citizen when we got to our assigned countries.

As Orientation progressed it became very clear that the personnel at 475 were not really interested in sending missionaries. To me, it seemed as if they were more interested in their pet subjects, such as racism, sexism, peace with justice, etc. While it wasn't stated, it seemed as if they would have preferred not to be bothered by sending missionaries, and instead, be free to concentrate on their particular areas of interest. One got the idea that they were fooling with us because, as a part of the Board, that was expected of them. But their heart wasn't in it.

Twice during the Orientation, we were asked to raise our hands to indicate what theological perspective we each held. Of the 33 candidates; 8 identified themselves as evangelicals", maybe 4 or 5 as "liberals", and the rest as "liberation theology". Of the 11 seminary-trained missionary candidates, those who would be in seminary or influential pastoral positions, 10 were liberation, and one was evangelical.

The motivation for going as missionaries varied greatly among the group. Some were interested in bringing about world peace, some wanted to free people from oppression, some were just interested in other cultures, some wanted to use their position as a stepping stone for getting their masters' degree, some felt called of God, and some simply wanted to help people.

One missionary in Patty's primary group said that his biggest problem in becoming a missionary and going overseas was what he should do with the girl he has been living with for the past year. Should he give her a ring or break up with her? When he expressed some genuine guilt for having had the relationship in the first place, a woman in the group interrupted him, "Why, you don't have anything to feel guilty about," she exclaimed. "We're sexual people; we all have to express ourselves somehow."

We were angered by the overwhelming liberation slant the Orientation had. Even the most liberal candidate commented on the lack of balance theologically. We felt our precious time was being wasted on political ideologies. We also resented being a captive audience for everyone in the World Division with a pet issue: racism, sexism, etc. For instance, we were told that because we were white we were automatically racist. PERIOD. No discussion. Being a racist resulted from our being white, and not from our attitudes and actions.

A great concern that we had about the personnel in the Africa Office was that as far as we knew, none of them, except Miss Patricia Rothrock, had any missionary experience beyond brief trips to Africa. We were being told how to be missionaries and what to expect by people who had never been missionaries themselves. We were told such things as, "Don't live in missionary compounds; live in the village with the people. Eat their food; be like them in every way. Don't have them work for you, etc." A missionary friend of ours who was raised in Zaire said that those who do such things not only get very sick very soon, but the nationals laugh at them for trying to be like them. A former missionary told Patty and me privately, "These guys don't know what they are doing."

From what I observed, people on the Board simply don't know what missionary life is like. As a result of this there is a gap between the personnel in the field and those at 475. The people in the field that I spoke with by-and-large find the Board a hindrance; a stone around the neck, and I can see why. We were more than a little uneasy when we realized that we would have to depend on these people should an emergency develop when we got to Africa.

We also found a disturbing lack of organization, communication and competence among the GBGM officials. We repeatedly received conflicting information regarding our assignment, For example, within a one-hour period, two officials from the Africa Office gave us two completely different job descriptions. No one could tell us for sure whether or not our future home had any electricity, whether water was available or not, and if we would have any transportation. This basic information was vitally important because we were going to a primitive and remote area 80 miles from any medical care. And, what is more frustrating, no one seemed interested in finding out for us, even after we made repeated inquiries. We ended up making several costly long distance calls to former missionaries from Sierra Leone to find out basic information, like what facilities were available, what to take, and what to expect in our future home. Methodism has had missionaries on the field for years. This Orientation and sending process should be down to a smooth-running, efficient operation by now, instead of the confusion and contradiction we experienced.

After the Orientation had ended we found we really knew little more about our assignment and what we should expect than we had known prior to it. I think the general feeling that I had was, "I've been cheated!" I gave up preaching at a Youth Institute that I very much wanted to do. What I got in return took three and a half weeks, but all that was applicable to us could have been done easily in one week.

My general impression, after several months to reflect on the whole affair, is that most of the personnel at 475 that I met were chosen on the basis of quota requirements instead of ability and experience. They seem to have little concern for the salvation of the lost, nor do they seem to have any concept of the uniqueness of Christ.

My personal opinion is that the Board is so involved in perpetuating itself and its programs that it has largely, if not totally, lost sight of why it exists at all. I firmly believe that any efforts at reform are going to meet with tremendous opposition at 475 (Riverside Drive, New York City). I have become convinced that our mission program, as it currently exists, is a dead body which doesn't know it yet. I came away from Orientation feeling very much like a kidney in a corpse, waiting anxiously to be transplanted before, I, too die.

After this experience I am convinced that the Mission Society for United Methodists is an absolute necessity, and that the GBGM will never be changed!

- Permission to print granted by The Rev. Max Borah, Duqoin, Illinois. In an interview, he stated that he does not believe the GBGM has changed.

Appendix J

Report To The GBGM Finance Committee

Sheraton Hotel
Stamford, Connecticut
March 22, 1992

When the 1988 General Conference authorized a task force of unbiased persons, lay and clergy, to study the feasibility of relocating the General Board of Global Ministries [GBGM] from its current location in New York City, I went back home from St. Louis feeling that the whole process would be handled with integrity. After all, the 15 persons on the task force were carefully selected by our bishops. There were 3 chosen from each of the 5 jurisdictions within the United States. All were strong church leaders, and I was fully confident that their findings would be those in the best interest of our church. I was also very pleased to learn later that 5 of the 15 persons selected by our bishops for this important task force were either past or present directors of the General Board of Global Ministries, thoroughly familiar with the present location of the headquarters in New York City.

The Task Force met on numerous occasions over the past four year. They hired the firm of Price Waterhouse to assist then in their study. These highly respected church leaders gave unselfishly hundreds of hours in studying the issue at hand. They spent approximately $70,000 fulfilling the task that our 1988 General Conference assigned them to do. After they completed their thorough research, the Task Force voted overwhelmingly that it was NOT ONLY FEASIBLE to move the GBGM out of New York City, but they also recommended that IT SHOULD BE MOVED. It is highly significant that 2 of the 3 representatives from the Northeastern Jurisdiction on the task force voted that it should be moved, minimizing the accusation that there was a regional prejudice.

While the General Conference Task Force was making their study, I can assure you that as Chairman of the GBGM Finance

Committee, I was prepared to accept whatever recommendation this group of highly qualified and conscientious persons brought forth. However, I learned very quickly that many of my colleagues on the executive staff at 475 Riverside Drive were not nearly as open. I could hardly believe my eyes when I discovered that certain of these staff persons were beginning to mobilize forces to discredit the findings of the Task Force long before the findings were even revealed. I heard arrogant, condescending voices regarding the workings of the Task Force, and I had a hard time correlating the criticisms of the Task Force with the fact that the 15 persons on the Task Force were carefully selected by our bishops and highly qualified. It then became apparent to me that the general Conference Task Force had not been shown the decency of having their report placed in the hands of the directors before there were powerful organized efforts to discredit their recommendation. As I listened and observed all of the unfair treatment directed toward the Task Force and the arrogant disregard of their recommendation, I decided that someone should have the "guts" to stand up and be counted. Be assured that I knew when I chose this course of action that I would have very few supporters among the 178 directors of the GBGM. However, I never dreamed that key executive staff at 475 Riverside Drive would go to such great extremes to mobilize forces against me and question my integrity.

While I continued to observe actions aimed at never giving the Task Force recommendation a fair hearing, I received a telephone call from Mr. Jim Steele, then editor of *The Christian Advocate* serving the Alabama-West Florida and North Alabama Conferences. He asked if I would write an article on "Why The GBGM Should Relocate from New York City." In an effort to off-set what I perceived to be an assassination of the Task Force Committee's report, I chose to write the article.

No sooner had the ink dried on my article did I become a target of vicious criticism. Just 30 minutes before I left home coming to this meeting, I received in the mail a letter that had been mailed to all directors with the names of the officers of the GBGM listed at the end. The letter blatantly accused me of using inaccurate information in my article. Upon arriving at our GBGM meeting here in

Stamford, Connecticut, I was shocked to learn that the very substance of the article was developed by Betty Thompson, staff member of GBGM at 475 Riverside Drive, with the encouragement of Randy Nugent and the assistance of his secretary, Rene Wilbur. After the Cabinet at 475 Riverside Drive had an opportunity to scrutinize the document, it was THEN mailed to the GBGM officers for their editorial revisions. As a matter of record, I want it clearly understood that this letter calling into question my integrity was basically written by a staff employee at 475 Riverside Drive who is totally opposed to relocation, and yet her name does not appear anywhere on the document.

In an effort for truth to reign supremely, I would like for those across the church to hear my side of the story. I challenge the news media (outside of 475 Riverside Drive) or any investigative reporter to check out my responses and allow all of the delegates to the 1992 General Conference to discern for themselves who is telling the truth.

I would like the sunshine of truth to break through on each of. the following issues where I was accused of providing inaccurate information.

I. Severance Package For Peggy Billings

In pointing out the wastefulness of the GBGM located in such an expensive environment, I pointed out in my article that "one executive who was terminated with the GBGM was given a severance package of $500,000 over 5 years." This one statement has created a storm of protest among the key executives at 475 Riverside Drive, so I hope and pray that the truth of this matter might be made clear to the whole world of United Methodism.

On May 13, 1988, 13 members of the Executive Committee of the World Division met in Denver, Colorado. One of the main issues addressed at that meeting was the fact that Peggy Billings, Deputy General Secretary of the GBGM, was not being renominated to her position. The minutes of that meeting in Denver contain these words,

"It was agreed to establish, upon completion of a contract satisfactory to Peggy Billings and the GBGM, an account in the amount of $300,000, to cover World Division commitment to the funding of the Project on the Church, Society and Ethics, to be paid out in terms of the contract. Source of funds: Collins Funds, in the category of administrative expenses of the World Division, one of the two categories for the use of Collins Funds agreed upon with the Collins family and designated by Directors: missionary retirement benefits and World Division Administration."

On May 21, 1988, the Executive Session of the Women's Division minutes include the following paragraph.

"Recommended:
1. That "The Church, Ethics, and Society Project Plan" be approved. It was voted.
2. That funding of the above PLAN be in the amount of $100,000 annually, for a 5 year period, with 40% paid by the Women's Division and the balance (60%) to be paid by the World Division; and that the source of funds for the Women's Division share be the Excess Deficit Fund. It was voted."

The United Methodist Reporter shared an article with its readers that was provided by the United Methodist News Service. It was headlined, "Two Global Ministries Executives Given New Church-Related Projects." Among other things the article states, "Two high-ranking officials of the United Methodist Church's General Board of Global Ministries who were not renominated to their position last spring will take on new church-related projects.... At its 1988 spring meeting, the board's personnel and nominating committee, in a closed door session as required by the *Book of Discipline* regarding personnel matters, decided against renominating the two executives for another term in the fall."

Regardless of how one seeks to explain the $500,000 (one-half million) appropriation over 5 years, the simple truth is that a staff member who was not renominated, or in my understanding "terminated" as head of a division was "given" a position that offered a "package" of $500,000 over 5 years. When I used the word "package," I also had in mind not only salary, but also pension, insurance, transportation costs, research, seminars, and other related costs pertaining to the project.

Yes, I was present in Denver, Colorado on May 13, 1988 when the initial action was taken. I did speak out at that meeting. I clearly recall that the only matter to be decided at that meeting was whether or not the $100,000 appropriation per year would be open-ended or limited to five years. The "wheels were greased" for the half-million allocation to support a person AND project, the recipient of which was one who had not been renominated as head of a division. One bishop on our Board that I highly respect explained this as a "sweetheart deal", but I think the the whole thing was sour and rotten to the core.

The Church and Society Project is now 3 years old, and I have not heard it mentioned the first time. Where is there a periodic progress report on the Project? How is the project progressing? What will be done with the final report? Will it be publicized for the GBGM to use? What contract was finally agreed upon as acceptable to the author and GBGM? Why was she not renominated to her position as Deputy General Secretary of the GBGM?

The overarching question that I would like to raise regarding the whole matter of severance for Peggy Billings and her project is simply this,

"HOW COULD AN APPROPRIATION OF THIS MAGNITUDE (ONE-HALF MILLION DOLLARS OVER 5 YEARS) BE GRANTED WITHOUT EVER BEING PRESENTED TO THE BOARD FINANCE COMMITTEE?"

The officers of the GBGM in their letter to all of the directors falsely allude that I did not raise the issue related to the severance pay and project at the May 13, 1988 meeting in Denver. That is incorrect. I raised the issue then, and I continued to raise the issue throughout the quadrennium.

On May 27, 1989, I received a letter from Harry A. Newman in Atlanta, then Field Representative for Mission Cultivation of the Southeastern Jurisdiction. Dr. Newman wrote,

"Rumor has it (and I certainly believe it to be true) that those who have been asked to resign from the GBGM during the past months have uniformly received significant cash settlements...

often reported to be in the nature of thousands and thousands of dollars. It seems a bit unusual to me that we are willing to reward those whom we have decided to replace because they are no longer fulfilling the needs of the organization while adopting in my own case a policy which penalizes me rather severely because of the unplanned and actually unavoidable death of my wife. My thinking may not be completely clear, but it seems to me that we are penalizing those who are still performing their duties in a completely satisfactory manner and rewarding those who have not done so."

On June 30, 1989, I wrote a letter to Mr. Steve Brimigion, GBGM treasurer, in which I stated among other things that it was very difficult for me as Chairman of Finance to explain to persons like Harry Newman the allocation of $500,000, regardless of the source of the funds. I asked Mr. Brimigion in my letter,

"Where does the Finance Committee fulfill its responsibilities for the receipt of the funds of the Board when these kinds of decisions are made by other persons or groups?"

I want to go on record once again as saying that no matter how one wants to explain the allocation of $500,000 to Peggy Billings for her salary, fringe benefits, project, and all related costs, the whole matter has a stench to it and is rotten to the core!

II. Cost Of Board Meetings:

The officers of the Board in their letter to the directors took issue with my figures pertaining to the cost of Board meetings. As we prepare to begin a new quadrennium, I would like to invite the readers of this article to carefully scrutinize the attached financial forms attributed by Mr. Steve Brimigion, GBGM treasurer, three years ago (1989), beginning a new quadrennium. This financial report includes exact financial figures expended in 1988.

Isn't it interesting that the 1988 spring, fall, and organizational meetings cost $1,039,000. Now we are saying that the Board will spend only $700,000 for two meetings in 1992.

Perhaps, a close scrutiny of the 1988 expenditures will shed light on why this kind of unrealistic low figure can be projected. While we spent $1,039,971 on three meetings in 1988, we had budgeted only $845,000.

You will also note many other items that greatly exceeded the budget. The General Secretary's TRAVEL in that one year was $64,052 with an appropriation of $50,000. When a member of our Board Finance Committee asked Steve Brimigion how this could happen, his response was, "Who am I to tell Randy that he cannot travel?"

Immediately following the meeting in which these figures were received, one of our new directors at that time, Elizabeth Gionti, wrote a letter to Mr. Steve Brimigion in which she included these words,

"Unless there is accountability at all levels of the organization which contributed to the $1,000,000 over budget for 1988, we surely are going to witness some mess! Even a quick perusal of the 22 page document of 1989 and 1990 appropriations for Board-wide Priorities, Meetings, General administration, Treasury, and Services shows exorbitant overspending on meetings plus travel and contingencies in just about every office from the General Secretary down. I would have thought that significant overspending in any area would require prior approval of at least the Finance Committee, if not the full Board of Directors."

As one reflects upon these figures, it is very obvious that United Methodists across the world have every right to be concerned about the budget controls at GBGM.

III. Size Of Board

The letter from the officers of the GBGM to all our directors makes note of the fact that "the General Conference, not the Board, has determined the size and composition of the GBGM." While that is true, be assured that our GBGM is a very powerful board with powerful influence at General Conference. If we were really serious about streamlining costs and providing more money for missions, we could easily go on record in support of petitions to General Conference limiting all Boards and Agencies to no more than 75 members. It is absolutely ludicrous that we have 178 members on our Board of Directors, some of which, oftentimes, come from the very same town and very same church.

Our GBGM cannot blame the General Conference for the multitude of committee meetings, duplication of services, and general wastefulness that permeates nearly every aspect of our Board.

IV. Cost Of Moving

The letter from the officers of the GBGM states that I express no concern at the cost of moving which has been estimated at figures from $9 to $15 million dollars. One of the significant points that the General Conference Task Force is seeking to make is that no matter what the cost, they are able to present facts and figures showing that the costs will be "recoverable".

When key leaders of GBGM learned that the General Conference Task Force recommended relocation, the arrogance of our Board was once again portrayed. Steps were taken immediately for us to request that GCFA and GCOM conduct an independent study. By our Board's action, it was decided that if GCFA and GCOM refused to do it, we would go ahead and pay for the $25,000 study. It should not surprise anyone that GCFA and GCOM refused to do it.

I would like to refresh the memories of all of our directors that the very last speech that Spurgeon Dunnam made on the floor at our October, 1991, meeting, he spoke about the sheer "arrogance" of our Board spending $25,000 for such a study. He alluded to the negative reaction this would have among our constituencies across the church, spending $25,000 for such a project while we are saying to the same people that we do not have sufficient funds for other purposes. I think Spurgeon Dunnam was prophetic in his remarks!

Although I, like Spurgeon Dunnam, was strongly opposed to the allocation of $25,000 for our own study, I asked Steve Brimigion, our treasurer to keep me as Finance Chairman abreast of any action regarding this study. On March 19, 1992, one day before coming to this spring meeting, I received in the mail a letter from Steve Brimigion, informing me that the general counsels of the church had declined the request of the GBGM to conduct a study of relocation costs. He then states in his letter,

"We have retained PHH Fantus Company as consultants to accurately estimate the cost of any move GBGM night have to make."

Who did the treasurer consult prior to hiring this firm? How are we to put any confidence in a $25,000 study made by a firm selected by persons adamantly opposed to relocation? When will the study be held? What purpose will it serve?

If the main reason for not relocating the GBGM is financial, would you not expect the Treasurer and General Secretary to at least consult the Chairman of the Board Finance Committee regarding our Board's response to the whole issue? I have never been asked by the Treasurer or General Secretary to be a part of any group chosen to respond to the report of the General Conference Task Force.

V. Jurisdictions From Which Staff Members Of GBGM Are Selected

The officers of GBGM take issue with my stating that the majority of the staff of the GBGM comes from the Northeast. I would like for the record to show that the Report of the General Conference Task Force states,

"Approximately 70% of the applicants for executive level positions and half of those employed in recent years have come from residents of the Northeastern Jurisdiction."

VI. "Out Of Touch" With Southeast

The officers of the GBGM attack my statement that the theological and philosophical persuasions of the staff at GBGM are far different or "out of touch" with those of us within the Southeast. Once again, I call to your attention an exact quote from the Task Force report,

"The New York City location is at one edge of the United States membership of the United Methodist Church which compounds the perception that it is theologically and philosophically remote from the mainstream of the United Methodist Church."

The one great proof of the fact that the GBGM is "out of touch" with the people of the Southeast can be clearly seen in the whole relocation issue. While upwards of 90% of the GBGM directors would probably vote against relocation, I will predict that the delegates from the Southeast will vote strongly in favor of relocation. Who are the strongest and loudest critics of the GBGM within the Alabama-West Florida Conference? Tragically enough, it is those former missionaries who have served unselfishly for many years under the auspices of the GBGM and now have grave misgivings about the actions of our GBGM.

The fact that the Southeastern Jurisdiction has traditionally been an enthusiastic supporter of missions speaks more of the faithful, generous people called United Methodists in our area fulfilling the mandate of Jesus Christ rather than strong support of the actions of GBGM.

VII. GBGM Hospitality At General Conference

The officers of the GBGM in their report take issue with my reference to "many, many thousands of dollars" that will be expended to "lobby" delegates at General Conference.

The unbelievable "lobbying" efforts on the part of the GBGM forces have already begun with letters having been sent to delegates all over the world. I have attended three previous General Conferences, and I have seen firsthand the powerful political pressure of the GBGM. I only want the "grassroots" of United Methodism to clearly understand in advance of General Conference that when the GBGM plans a huge reception for delegates in one of the most expensive hotels in Louisville, they are creating an "unequal playing field" in an atmosphere where important decisions are to be made. It will be terribly, terribly difficult for particular delegates who are beholden to the GBGM and staff for funding to resist the pressure that the lobbying forces of GBGM will put upon them regarding the relocation issue.

What will be the cost of the reception? What will be the source of these funds?

Closing Personal Statement:

I am presently serving in my ninth year as pastor of the First United Methodist Church of Montgomery, Alabama. During those nine years, our church has been recognized by our Conference Board of Missions for having given more money to United Methodist missions through Advance Specials than any of the 720 churches of the Alabama-West Florida Conference. We have within our church what I feel is the strongest United Methodist Women's organization of any church within our Conference. I have never served a church that did not pay 100% of its World Service and Conference Benevolences. Within the past few weeks, two GBGM missionaries have spoken from our pulpit where I am privileged to speak each Sunday. On May 24, 1992, Tim and Carol Crawford, GBGM missionaries to Mozambique, will speak in our church. Last weekend, our church hosted the Cuban Shalom Choir that sang in our church on three occasions and spent two nights in the homes of our church members. It was a marvelous experience for us! Our church during the past year has sent Volunteers in Mission teams to Costa Rica and Jamaica. I have been down in the front line trenches as a District Superintendent, strongly encouraging members of local churches to support all of the United Methodist mission programs. I have spoken for our United Methodist Women on a local, district, and conference basis, strongly supporting their gifts to missions.

I have served as President of the Alabama-West Florida Conference Council of Finance and Administration, as well as Chairman of the Council on Finance and Administration for the Southeastern Jurisdiction. Never in all of my life has my integrity been called into question by stating that I provided "inaccurate information." Since my integrity has been called into question, I would love for the news media (outside 475 Riverside Drive) to let the light of truth shine upon each of these matters contained in my article.

I must return home tomorrow to officiate at the funeral of one of our most faithful members, Roonie Gentry. I deeply regret that I will be unable to stay for the remainder of our spring board meeting to defend myself from any other attacks upon my truthfulness.

As I come to my final general board meeting after serving on this Board for 8 years, I must confess that it has been a very disillusioning experience. I have experienced a very difficult time as a local pastor seeing widows on fixed income giving sacrificially to the mission programs of our great church while at the same time as chairman of the Board Finance Committee knowing that we appropriated $500,000 for a person and project when that very person had not been renominated as the Deputy General Secretary of the World Division. I have equally been disillusioned by 178 directors spending over $300,000 for a week's meeting in New York City and the sheer arrogance of appropriating $25,000 for our own study for relocation that flies in the face of the one authorized by the General Conference.

Although Don Messer and I do not agree on the issue of relocation, I think that he is right on target when he says that as a GBGM, "We can win the battle and lose the war!" I do not know how the final vote will be in Louisville on the matter of relocation. My life and ministry will not be changed one way or the other if the Board does not relocate. However, I want to go on record as saying that if this GBGM continues to arrogantly resist General Conference mandated task force recommendations such as the one regarding relocation, you can rest assured that the World Service dollars will continue to drop all across the world of United Methodism.

Thanks for listening!

Dr. Karl K. Stegall, Chairman
General Board of Global Ministries
Finance Committee

Appendix K

Financial Report on The United Methodist General Board of Global Ministries

The following is a financial snapshot of The (UM) General Board of Global Ministries (GBGM) that was contained in "The 1997 Stewardship Report on The United Methodist Church"*. The information presented here is far from comprehensive; a shortage of space precludes our giving more complete coverage and analyses of expenditures by the GBGM. Since this board is designated by the United Methodist Church's *Book of Discipline* as the "missional instrument" of the UMC, it has a primal responsibility to translate God's commands into practice. The largest agency in the UMC, it receives more money than does any other. In the examination of financial data, it should be noted that there have been discrepancies between the Treasurer's Report (TR) and the unaudited Financial Disclosure Report (FDR), both of which are published by the GBGM; these are the primary source documents used in all of our financial studies of this organization. For instance (for historical purposes), income differences varied from the greatest in 1992 (TR): $120,467,706 versus FDR: $134,326,668 - a difference of $13,858,962, or 11.50%) to the least in 1994 (TR): $133,173,640 versus FDR: $133,770,208 - a difference of $596,568, or .448%). For the sake of consistency, FDR figures were used since this is the document that also lists organizations supported.

	1994	1995	1996
GBGM Assets:	$295,956,199	$387,994,505	$409,210,898
% Change of assets from Previous Year:	2.06% Decrease	31.10% Increase	5.47% Increase

| GBGM Income: | $133,770,208 | $168,847,907 | $191,551,170TR |
| % Change of income from Previous Year: | 15.56% Increase | 26.22% Increase | 13.358% Increase |

| Administration/NYC Office Support: | $30,226,708 | $32,668,817 | $49,486,777 |
| % of GBGM Budget: | 22.65% | 19.35% | 25.835% |

| Direct Spt./Persons in Mission (GBGM): | $16,392,710 | $22,731,586 | $19,241,794 |
| % of GBGM Budget: | 12.25% | 13.46% | 10.045% |

| Direct Spt./Pers. in Mission (World Div.): | $11,361,989 | $15,572,143 | $10,787,894 |
| % of GBGM Budget: | 8.49% | 9.22% | 5.632% |

A full board meeting costs $350,000, while executive committee meetings cost $275,000. The GBGM spent $738,000 for two meetings in 1995 and had budgeted $855,785 for two in 1996.(See Appendix J, "Report by Dr. Karl Stegall") For 1996, the General Board of Global Ministries had net assets of $409,210,898, more than at any other time in its history. The GBGM received $191,551,170 in revenues in 1996, up from $168,847,907 in 1995 - an increase of $22,703,263, or +13.358%. Of 1996's total income, $22,900,588 came from World Service apportioned funds,

$39,989,923 from the Women's Division funds and from the United Methodist Women, and the rest from outside trusts and interest, dividends, capital gains from the GBGM's some $273,517,812 of investments in 1996 (up from $251,729,019 in 1995).

Support of the GBGM's offices in New York City and other administrative expenses received $49,486,777 (25.83% of income), up from $32,668,817 in 1995 (19.35% of income for that year). In contrast, direct support of persons in mission received $19,241,794 in 1996 (10.045% of income), down from $22,731,586 in 1995, which was 13.46% of income for that year. Direct support of persons in mission in the world division [i.e., foreign missionaries] was $10,787,894 in 1996 (5.632% of income), down from $15,572,143 in 1995 (9.22% of income for that year). This is consistent with the pattern of decline of money actually reaching the mission field, not only for the World Division but for the entire GBGM as well.[This correlates with the experiences of Dr. Julia McLean Williams in her testimony "So Great a Cloud" in Appendix N] In the past, American Methodism fielded over 2500 in the 1920s, far more than any other Protestant denomination. By the 1960s it had declined to 1500, and to 516 in 1985, 323 in 1993, 320 in 1995, and to the present total of 287 (foreign) missionaries with the World Division. Citing "budget problems" for 1993 and 1994, Robert J. Harman, World Division Executive stated that 20 missionaries "must retire or not continue in missionary service" due to reduced funding[1], yet despite the fact that total revenues received by the GBGM are higher than ever before, the missionary force has dwindled to the present level.

The financial data above reflect the picture that overall revenues have been increasing, and more money is going to the category of "administrative expenses" (to include support of its offices in New York City), both in actual dollars and also as a higher percentage of GBGM income. This latter statistic reflects a double increase since higher proportions of a growing revenue are allocated to this area. On the other hand, money allocated into overall mission support and foreign mission support decreased, both in terms of real dollars and in terms of the percentage of GBGM revenues.

The study [by The Rev. Ed Ezaki, CPA, and former Member of the Audit and Review Committee of the General Council on Finance and Administration (GCFA)] included in Appendix L approaches the stewardship issue from the perspective that GCFA policy is that denominational agencies retain a minimum of 25% of annual operating budgets in reserve. If this is the case, the figures cited above show excessive accumulation of moneys at the general church level. This study then offers the estimate that the World Division of the GBGM has accumulated assets representing 40 years' worth of World Service Fund income. In other words, with the funds it has invested, it could operate for 40 more years without receiving another penny from the World Service part of the apportionments. In addition, the fact that our general boards and agencies have accumulated more invested assets now than at any other time in history is indicative that not all of the money given in response to appeals, based on poignant pictures showing abject need, is making its way to help the people so portrayed. In other words, the pictures are used to elicit sympathy on the part of donors, who give their money thinking it will alleviate that poverty, but the funds are invested by the general agencies and they become wealthier.

Observations.

- Money ($442,004) allocated in the Financial Disclosure Report indicated "Undesignated/No description found/Payee name not found." Although evidences of this were found in the past, the figure given here is for 1994 only. At best, this indicates a lack of financial responsibility in this money being expended with no record of the payee, nor a record of the cause for which the money was paid; at worst, this would be an obfuscation of the recipient to preclude disclosure. The World Division was by far the worst offender in this area with 3.63% of its moneys being used in this way.

- At present, the "mainline denominations" account for only 9% of all of missionaries sent out to foreign countries. [2]

- More money is spent on supporting the personnel and headquarters in New York City (a city that is one of the highest cost of living areas in the United States and the world) than on the entire missionary force: total expenditures on administration and support of the NYC office for 1996 was $49,486,777, while support of persons in overseas mission totaled $10,787,894. The support of the NYC offices and other administrative expenses is 4.587 times that of the entire overseas missionary force. This reflects "overhead expense" in supporting the overseas missionary force.

- On keeping the GBGM in New York, A UM Teenager had wanted the GBGM to move to Independence, Kansas where the Atlantic Richfield Company had offered a free 140,000 square-foot building. Cody Nuss, 18, appealed the decision of the site Selection Task Force to consider only Atlanta, Chicago, Dallas, Denver, and Washington, D.C., but met with no results. Don Messer chaired the task force.[3] An amendment to consider a move to the Atlanta area was defeated. Ignoring the Price-Waterhouse estimate of $9-12 million dollars for the cost of the move and using the GBGM-commissioned study of $72 million, the 1996 General Conference voted to explore remaining in New York City, to be decided at the year 2000 General Conference. (See Appendix J "Report by Dr. Karl Stegall")

- The GBGM continues to espouse radical ideas such as "liberation theology" (the theology of some movements which espouse violence to achieve their goals) while eschewing traditional biblical Christianity. In conversation, a top GBGM executive was told by one of his missionaries that "an experience with Jesus Christ was a necessity to be a good missionary;" the executive's reply was, "That's a controversial statement." When questioned by a candidate for the foreign mission field about evangelism, another GBGM staffer stated, "Oh, we don't convert anyone to Christ; we let God do that" (see Appendix I "Missionary Orientation"). A dominant view is that to try to evangelize others is "to exhibit the height of spiritual arrogance" or "spiritual imperialism.

- In the area of political Activism, at its Fall 1994 directors' meeting, the GBGM called for friendlier U.S. ties with communist Cuba and North Korea. In addition to its promised support for the WCC investigation of alleged human rights abuses in the U.S., it donated $50,000 to the WCC for support of its investigation.[4] At its Spring, 1995 meeting, the GBGM called for U.S. relations with (communist) North Korea, the withdrawal of U.S. forces from South Korea, the promotion of Korean reunification, and the recognition of the U.S. role in "perpetuating the suffering and separation of the Korean people." GBGM representative Lois Dauway Supported President Clinton's veto of the Partial Birth Abortion bill. At its April directors meeting, the GBGM denounced Republican ideas as "mean-spirited" and established a "Human Welfare Crisis Task Force" to resist congressional budget cuts. A delegation from the board's Women's Division will lobby Congress directly. Division chief Joyce Sohl claims there "are many demons in our midst today" as she bemoaned a "reshifting of national priorities towards military preparedness" and away from "children's health and education." Both the GBGM and the bishops oppose cuts in welfare programs.[5]

- The 1996 GBGM's Financial Disclosure Report has seen a marked increase of money given to organizations involved in various aspects of universal health advocacy, political activism, "women's theology," "day care," "environmental racism," "economic justice," "economic racism," and "justice" issues. There is concern that money spent on the "women's theology" may, in fact, be used to promote the "goddess" theologies evident at the 1993 "Re-Imagining" Conference. It is thought that this advocacy works toward a society in which all have equal pay, standards of living, etc., which would, in turn, devolve to a "classless" society.

(The) Women's Division (WD) of the General Board of Global Ministries:

Insight: "The hand that rocks the cradle steadies the Nation." A comment by J. E. McFayden is cogent, and Amos 4:1-3 provides a case in point: "All the Hebrew prophets knew that for the temper and quality of a civilization, the women are greatly responsible. A country is largely what its women make it; if they are careless or unworthy, the country is on the road to ruin." - The Navigators

The Women's Division (WD) is a dynamic, capable part of the GBGM. Its revenue-generating skills would be the envy of any fund-raising organization in the country, and much of its money goes to support good causes. Unfortunately, some finds its way into questionable use; misleading rhetoric further clouds the reality of its ultimate destination. For instance, many fund raising activities are used to raise money to go directly into "missions," with visions of support provided to feed a "hungry child" or to care for a "poverty-stricken family." But in reality, this money goes into one of several funds comprising the WD's over $100,000,000 in assets. From there it is channeled into any number of causes, some of which are listed in this study. Further confusing the issue is an imprecise definition of the term "missions." Traditionally, evangelicals understand it to mean caring for the physical needs of people coupled with attempts to lead them into a saving relationship with Jesus Christ. Money raised by UM tithes and other fund-raising activities may be used to support true missions, but it is more likely that it will go to something entirely different: from providing sociopolitical services for people to funding attendance at events such as the "Re-Imagining" Conference.

Following is an examination of funding for the Women's Division for the most current three years:

	1994	1995	1996
WD Assets:	$92,911,935	$108,991,817	$110,983,970
WD Income:	$34,341,262	$52,471,182	$39,989,923

Income was significantly larger in 1995 than 1994, an increase of 52.79%. Despite the fact that funding decreased from 1995 to 1996, it is still greater than in 1994. The Women's Division is reflective of other general boards by growing its accumulated investments.

*   *   *

"Read it and weep. Weep for the millions of families and children who could have been saved from starvation and disease. Weep for the millions who might have been saved for heaven but were not. Weep for our trusting members who have apparently been fleeced for several years by the General Board of Global Ministries in their ignorance and greed. Weep for our pastors who have been intimidated for years by District Superintendents and Bishops who threatened removal to pastors who told the truth to their congregations. This is intolerable."
- The Rev. Dan Lauffer, pastor, formerly of FUMC, Prophetstown, Illinois

Unless otherwise noted, data above came from the following:
- *Report of the Treasurers of the General Board of Global Ministries* for the years covering 1994, 1995, and 1996.
- *Financial Disclosure Report of the General Board of Global Ministries of the United Methodist Church* for the years 1994, 1995, and 1996.
- *The Daily Christian Advocate for the General Conference of the United Methodist Church*, covering the 1997-2000 quadrennium.

Notes:
1. Speech by Dr. Gerald Anderson, CONVO 90 in Louisville, Kentucky.
2. *The United Methodist Reporter*, November 5, 1993, p. 3.
3. *Newscope*, September 2, 1994, p. 2.
4. See Annex G of "The 1997 Stewardship Report on The United Methodist Church" on the Concerned Methodists' website*
5. *UMAction Briefing*, Spring 1995, p. 1.
* Available on the INTERNET at the Concerned Methodists website at: "http://cmpage.org"

Appendix L

UM Global Agencies Amass $100's of Millions in Excess Funds
by the Reverend Edward F. Ezaki, CPA
Member of the Audit
and Review Committee of the
General Council on
Finance and Administration of
The United Methodist Church

Source: The 1996 United Methodist Treasurer's Report

The 1996 United Methodist Treasurer's Report contains certain items which are most significant, especially in light of the continuous demands made upon the local church to pay 100% of its apportionments. The need for the apportionments to be paid 100% was in order that the General church might supply more missionaries, feed more starving children and reach more persons with the message of Jesus Christ. In exercising responsible stewardship within their local churches, pastors and lay people have the right to expect the church boards, agencies and educational institutions which are the beneficiaries of our giving to likewise exercise responsible stewardship. Thus you might find reason to be dismayed with the items mentioned below, which are extracted from the 1996 United Methodist Treasurer's Report.

Currently, GCFA has an approved policy that agencies retain a minimum of 25% of annual operating budget in reserve. Current levels of reserves (net assets) held by many agencies are excessive to the point of embarrassment to the General Church. The high levels of such reserves and the positive assets revealed by current audits of the General Church's financial statements have caused one auditor to remark that if The United Methodist Church were a corporation, "we would declare a dividend."

High levels of net assets raise serious questions about the stewardship practices of United Methodist general agencies. Stewardship entails more than the safeguarding of net assets. It also concerns the best use of such assets. Jesus' parable of the rich man who stored up riches in new barns (Luke 12) comes to mind. It is natural to question whether the accumulation of excessive net assets does not come at the expense of current investment in the mission of the Church. Unless the maintenance of high net asset levels compared to annual revenues are pursuant to explicit future needs, many within the Church will conclude that the wealth of the agencies is the goal.

It is difficult to support good faith appeals to local churches to pay World Service and other apportionments when the agencies are perceived to be more wealthy than the churches. Furthermore, it is misleading to promote apportionment giving as missional when substantial amounts of revenue are being retained in marketable securities, employee loans, and other investments at the agencies. It is also detrimental to donor morale when apportionment revenue becomes a minor funding source for an agency. When investment gain and income exceeds apportionment revenue, donors may feel that their giving is immaterial.

If the accumulation of net assets by general agencies allows for investment gains and other non-apportionment income streams to fund the majority of the agency's operations, the agency's financial reliance on connectional accountability is diminished. Unless the General Conference intends to create self-funded endowments for the general agencies, the desirability of such endowment is in question.

Among the findings uncovered in a recent independent analysis of the 1996 Treasurer's Report:

1. The World Division of the General Board of Global Ministries is the largest of the pre-1997 divisions making up the GBGM. Its total net assets as of 12/31/96 were $170,648,809. This is 3.3 times its annual $52 million revenue. Excluding the permanent reserve of $60,328,349, the total of unrestricted and temporary reserves are $110,320,460. There are some non-liquid type items

in the reserve balance ($374,019 in fixed assets, $37.2 million in the Collins Forest and $13 million in accrued post retirement benefits), yet the liquid reserves are close to $100 million. This level of net assets represents an increase of $21,272,306 (14.2%) over the prior year, an increase of $96,742,517 (131%) over the past four years. The World Division holds $132,279,906 in cash and marketable securities alone as of 12/31/96, over 31 times the annual World Service Fund income.

Perhaps the single most conclusive evidence that the net asset balance is excessive is that of total revenue in 1996 of $51,979,213, only $4.3 million comes from the World Service apportionment while close to $25 million comes from investment income and gain on investments. The World Division comes close to being self-funded. Its net assets based on 1996 levels represent 40 years worth of World Service Fund income.

2. The National Division of the General Board of Global Ministries had total net assets of $41,447,922 as of 12/31/96, $22 million of which is in non-permanent reserves. Cash and marketable securities of $28,421,558 produced investment income and gain of $4,199,521, almost the same amount as the $4,254,659 received from the World Service Fund. Total net assets as of 12/31/96 represent over 9.7 years of apportionment income.

3. The total of net assets for the largest divisions of the General Board of Global Ministries (World, National, Women's, and MPS) as of 12/31/96 are $335,102,291. The net assets of these divisions have increased 61% in the past four years. $93,620,694 of all this total is permanent reserve, leaving $241,481,597 in unrestricted and temporarily restricted net assets. $30,767,890 is received by these divisions from the World Service Fund and Women's Division allocations. The total non-permanent reserves represent 7.8 years worth of apportionment/allocation income. If net assets for these four divisions has to fund its apportionments and allocations, it could do so for over 11 years exclusive of any earnings on its investments.

4. The General Board of Church and Society had net assets as of 12/31/96 of $15,622,476. The GBCS's total reserve represents 5.8 years of World Service Fund allocation at current levels. The net assets total has increased 42% over the past four years. The cash and investments of $12,400,027 produce $1,935,412 in rental and investment income while the World Service apportionment income is $2,702,701. Thus, the reserve balances are functioning as an endowment for the Board.

5. The General Board of Higher Education and Ministry had net assets as of 12/31/96 of $75,807,672. of which $74,543,718 were not permanently restricted. This is an increase of $8,032,630 (11.9%) over the prior year. Total revenues are $30,382,329 of which $21,298,639 is from the World Service and Ministerial Education Funds. The GBHEM could continue at current levels for 3.6 years without these two apportioned income items. Evidence of excessive reserves is indicated in that the GBHEM has designated $31,547,806 of its reserves "for loans and scholarships," yet only has $8,510,539 in student loans outstanding and spends $2.8 million on program services for the Office of Loans and Scholarships. There seems no logical connection between the designated reserve and the actual level of loans and scholarships. This appears to indicate that the Board sees these designated reserves as an endowment.

6. The General Commission on Archives and History is a smaller agency which nonetheless has accumulated over one year's worth of net assets. Total net assets are $818,602. Over the past four years, the net assets have increased by 41%.

7. The General Board of Discipleship is the one agency included in the comparison which has less than one year's revenue in net assets (it has 93% of annual revenues in net assets). It is included for comparative purposes. Note that GBOD's investment income and gain is less than 3% of its annual revenue and is only 13% of apportionment revenue. However, even GBOD has experienced a 35% increase in net revenues over the past four years. At that rate, it is accumulating net assets in excess of revenue growth.

As you can imagine, these figures are most upsetting. Remember that they are extracted from the 1996 Report of the Treasurer, an official publication of The United Methodist Church. Therefore, the facts and figures quoted above are correct. Persons not familiar with discernment of complicated financial reports could not derive the information quoted above from the normal cursory glance most of us give to such reports. Because the Treasurer's Report is so complicated this information does not filter down to the local church. However, with the release of these very simple statements which un-complicate the Treasurer's Report, the local church will become informed.

The above report was originally taken from the "Unofficial Confessing Movement Page" on the INTERNET [http:// ucmpage.org] and is contained in the "1997 Stewardship Report on the United Methodist Church" published by Concerned Methodists, Inc. Permission granted to use this material.

The Reverend Edward F. Ezaki, who at the time this report was written was a member of the California-Nevada Conference, has since resigned as a member of the Audit and Review Committee of the General Council on Finance and Administration of The United Methodist Church.

Appendix M

Case Study: So Great A Cloud
by Dr. Julia McLean Williams

Dr. Julia McLean Williams served for 10 years as a United Methodist General Board of Global Ministries (GBGM) missionary to Bolivia in community development and Christian Education. She has directed some 16 mission teams to South America. Currently she serves as Executive vice President of the Mission Society for United Methodists.

When Convo 1990 was in the planning stage, I was invited to come and tell the story of my own personal journey in the church and missions. Mine is both a story of God's call upon an ordinary life to be obedient to the Great Commission and a story of the mission of the Church.

I grew up in a parsonage home in the Louisiana Conference. We moved every four or five years - as was the custom then - from North Louisiana to South Louisiana and places in between. There were seven children in Slim and Lucille McLean's family. I was one of the twins, born at home while my Daddy was attending annual conference. When we drove into any new town on moving day in the month of November, we were the social event of the season. Everyone was certain that seven children would wreck the parsonage, but they soon calmed down when they found out what kind of housekeeper Mama was. Of course, it didn't hurt that we filled up at least two rows in church and that as time went on, those who were "just friends of the family" increased church attendance, the church roll and its financial resources.

We heard about what Daddy and Mama expected of us and what God expected of us at home and in the church. We learned early on that, even with our own big family and the larger one of the local congregation, we were just a small part of an even larger family that lived around the world. From the big, soft Bible beside the dining table we learned about the kingdom of God. At night when we went to bed we heard stories from a thick, illustrated book, *Hulbert's Stories of the Bible,* and discovered what happens to ordinary people when they become God's people.

One Sunday Daddy invited a bishop from Mexico to speak at our church. He ate Sunday dinner with us. Between my plate and his was a lone English pea on the starched tablecloth. He pointed to it, winked and said, "Mine? or yourrrrrs?" It was then that I heard for the first time the trilled "r"s of the language I would one day learn in order to share the message of Christ in Bolivia, South America.

On Wednesdays after school the World Friendship Circle met in our parlor. Present at every meeting was a giant map with mysterious names all over it.

Nurture

Seven days a week the church nurtured our lives for service in that world. Wednesday night prayer meeting was as essential to our health as the spoon of black strap molasses Mama gave us every night. I remember the first prayer meeting at the last church Daddy served in New Iberia, Louisiana. It was moving day. Daddy had been transferred from Crowley, Louisiana, just 25 miles away, in one of those mid-year moves caused by a death in the conference. We arrived just in time for a quick supper and then ran next door to the church to meet our new church family. Daddy was the last one to arrive. He had hastily unpacked and changed into his new seersucker suit from Sears Roebuck. As he lifted his well-worn Bible to read the Scripture, there dangling from the button on his sleeve was the price [tag] of his new suit. My sister and I, both college students, broke into gales of laughter. Daddy stopped and asked what was so funny, and then joined our laughter; the congregation followed.

I learned a lot from my preacher Daddy: his view of the world and of his Heavenly Father, the value he placed on the Scripture and the place of prayer in his life. I was deeply affected by the way he serenely met the complexities of a minister's life.

And then there was Mama. She was his help in his work and was a giant in her own right! After I had become a missionary, she went with me back to where Daddy had served when I was six years old to hear me speak. Mama came into the church after the prelude had begun. When the people recognized her, they all rose from their seats to hug her and to applaud her presence. Her arrival literally broke up the service. She was a great woman.

My faith was nurtured by Daddy and Mama and by all those precious souls who faithfully shared our church life in Franklinton, Vivian, Bastrop, Crowley and New Iberia, Louisiana. Daddy had great expectations for me and for all his children. He expected us to continue to grow spiritually and to serve the Lord he served. In my first Bible he wrote the verse: "Study to show thyself approved unto God, a workman that needeth not to be ashamed" (2 Timothy 2: 15a, KJV).

Daddy died just two weeks before I graduated from college. He went home one Sunday in May after preaching a communion service and died of a heart attack. In his pocket we found these words written on a used envelope:

"Some Other hands by love inspired
And gifted for the task
Will reap the harvest in my stead
What more could mortals ask?"

Twenty years later Mama died, holding my hand and my sister's, talking to us about our families and to God about being ready to be with Him.

Heritage
No story about my journey could be complete without recognizing the heritage of faith I received through Mama, Daddy and that group of faithful servants in those churches who took seriously the command of Christ. They made sure not only that I heard his command but that I understood it as well.

Scripture
The words of Hebrews 12:1-2a come alive to me today because of them. These verses honor our heritage and unite us with

157

those who have gone before. The testimony of those who have gone before us challenges us to be obedient. Think about those around you here at Convo 1990 as you reflect on these words:

> Therefore, since we are surrounded by such a great cloud of witnesses, let us throw off everything that hinders and the sin that so easily entangles, and let us run with perseverance the race marked out for us. Let us fix our eyes on Jesus, the author and perfecter of our faith, who for the joy set before him endured the cross..." (Hebrews 12:1-2a).

You and I are those whom God calls to do his work in our time. We came here to Convo 1990 to reaffirm the imperative of world evangelization and to renew our own commitment to this task as we enter the decade of the 1990s.

My Story

Perhaps my story can be helpful as we look at what it means to lay aside every encumbrance. Laying aside encumbrances means to be set free of entangling sin within ourselves and our church. It means being able to run, not only with endurance but with the joy Jesus knew, the race before us. That race is the mission of the Church!

During this convocation several prominent bishops and outstanding United Methodist pastors of our great church have inspired us. But I come as a layperson. I represent the millions of United Methodists who look to our bishops, our pastors and our church to nurture and guide us. We live out our Christian faith from the pews, the Sunday School rooms, the vacation church schools, the mission studies, the United Methodist Women's groups, the neighborhood prayer fellowships and the places across this land where we minister outside the doors of the church.

My roles in the United Methodist Church since those early days of being nurtured in a parsonage have been many. I've served as a Sunday school teacher, youth leader, choir member and UMW member. I studied missions at Scarritt, went to Costa Rica to learn Spanish and served as a missionary for the Board of Global Ministries to

Bolivia, South America. I have led work teams to Central and South America and have interpreted the mission of the church as a core interpreter for the World Division. I organized Volunteers In Mission in the North Carolina Conference and taught missions in local churches at both conference and jurisdictional levels. On one occasion I was named Layperson of the Year in the North Carolina Conference. I have been Dean of the VIM rally at Lake Junaluska, and served five years as President of the Board of Missions in the North Carolina Conference. Since 1985 I have served on the Dialogue Committee mandated by General Conference in 1984. Now I am Chief Operations Officer of The Mission Society for United Methodists. With 61 years under my belt, I've done a lot!

Each of these roles placed me in direct and close contact with the lay people I represent. I want to show you who they are and share some of our thinking for the decade ahead of us. My twin brother, Jim McLean, professor of art at Georgia State University and a former United Methodist pastor, drew some cartoons to illustrate; I think you will recognize yourself and your church friends in them.

Ed and Eva Earnest just had their first baby. Even before he was born they began to realize that for their child to be well and happy it really matters not only what they believe but what the world believes. Since they wanted the best of life for their child and needed help, they took him to church on a bright Sunday morning to have him dedicated to God in baptism. The minister asked them some pointed questions on how they would "exercise all godly care" that he be brought up in the Christian faith, be taught the Holy Scriptures and attend church.

They heard those who stood with them say that with God's help, they would order their lives after the example of Christ and endeavor to live so that he could grow in the knowledge and love of God the Father through the Savior Jesus Christ. Eva left wondering if everybody really meant what they said-including themselves!

Malcolm Mediamania is a teenager. He has a hard time getting excited about Christianity-or even hearing about it since his ears and eyes are full of so many things that seem more fun. Most of the adults he knows in church don't seem too excited about it. He goes bowling and to Pizza Hut on Sunday night with the youth, and sometimes they even do a car wash to raise money for a retreat at the beach.

Rita Retired was a school teacher. She now teaches the third grade Sunday school, sits on the third row on the left-hand side of the church and smiles with pride when one of her former students sings a solo. She belongs to the night circle and faithfully pays her pledge each year to the United Methodist Women. She has a hard time with the study books at UMW and usually uses Guideposts or a friend who has been on a trip when it's her time to do the program.

William Wineheart Woe-is-Me ushers every Sunday. His wife insists. He has never voted "yes" on any program of the church and feels missions are a waste since there's enough to do here at home. He really likes the Methodist Men though because they discuss bird hunting and the basketball team. As his head gets balder, his mouth gets bigger.

Grandma Good-as-Gold is an inspiration. She is the one the preacher can ask to pray out loud without notifying her ahead of time. She carries her offering neatly folded in a clean handkerchief and never misses a service. She is a Bible scholar. Everyone loves and respects Grandma but seldom stops to ask why.

Broderick Busy is an extremely successful engineer. He is always tied up-always on his way to or from somewhere-and knows three languages. He is a world citizen and has lived in several countries. He is efficient and smart. If he is feeling really benevolent or guilty, he can sit through an entire budget meeting at the church.

Sam and Sally Singles sit on opposite ends of the pew every Sunday. Sam is divorced; Sally is an unwed mother. They come to church regularly to heal their wounds and search for the love that has somehow escaped them. It is better than the "Y" or a singles bar.

Mr. and Mrs. All American and their children, **Smart** and **Popular**, come to church on Sunday morning-a "picture book" family. They feel very safe in the church and we feel very safe when the pews are full of them. There is not a spot of dirt on them, and their sins are clean, perfumed and color coordinated!

Susan Singout is a choir member. We all know what Susan Singout and other choir members give to the life of the church! It is wonderful. I was in a church recently where the choir folks seemed too important. They sang specials and had presentations until seven minutes until 12:00. After hearing the sermon I realized they could have used six more minutes. If we want to know how to manage the church, we should go to the choir room.

Bertha Bureaucrat is a verbose, efficient United Methodist woman. She has followed instructions for the past 20 years, has boycotted everything she was told to and her collar is usually heavy with all kinds of pins she has been awarded for her faithfulness. When she is asked to pray, she reads it right off page 14 of the resource book.

Margaret and Mevil Mall Walker are pillars of the church. They are faithful with their presence and their pledge as they are with their laps around the mall. They aren't quite sure of what Bertha means when she says boycott Shell Oil since their son-in-law owns a Shell Station and doesn't have a mean bone in his body. They love their preacher and always tell him his sermon was good, even if they slept through it.

So great a cloud of witnesses-all kinds of people. In some we recognize ourselves or someone in the church we attend. There are lots of others:

* the chronically ill
* the elderly huddled around a TV
* the young mother who just lost her baby
* the 60-year-old man who married his 30-year-old secretary
* the wife he left
* the dying and

on and on, all sitting beside us right here and now. As the Scripture says, "Therefore, since we are surrounded by such a great cloud of witnesses, let us throw off everything that hinders" (Hebrews 12:1). What stands in the way? What encumbrances do we need to lay aside?

The first place we need to look is at ourselves as evangelical Christians. Now here is one perception of who we are. I know you recognize him. I call him **Dr. Cash-and-carry Kingdom Builder.** Sometimes we leaders in the evangelical community appear to be building our own kingdoms rather than the kingdom. We are notorious for our ego development and for doing "our own thing" even to the detriment of the causes we believe in most. The population of "Cash-and-carries" increases simply by saying, "The Lord told me to do it," which of course justifies everything-or anything.

Finally, there is the "angelic" crowd, the encumbering perfect, "holier-than-thous" who are extremely pious. We think we're just wonderful-and we are of course-but sometimes we act like the only ones who know anything.

As people of God whose eyes are fixed on Jesus, let us lay aside these and any other encumbrances we in this community of faith carry!

I must tell you, and I do it with sadness, that there are many encumbrances in my journey. When I returned from the mission field in 1969, I went straight to the conference office and told them I was a returned missionary and that I wanted to volunteer to help promote missions in my conference. It was fully two years later when the Conference Council on Ministries director called on me to serve, and then only because he accidentally scheduled himself in two places at the same time.

After that, things began to happen. He asked me if I would consider starting a Volunteers In Mission program like the one in the Holston and Western Carolina Conferences. We organized it and conducted five months of training and orientation. The first team went out from Edenton Street Church, the largest United Methodist Church in the conference. It was a huge success! All across the conference the people in the pew began to get excited about being Christians. They were being called on to testify to their faith, to pray and to rely on God. Everyone wanted to go. Not surprisingly, Advance Special giving nearly doubled.

One night when I arrived at a North Carolina beach for a team's orientation, I received a call from a minister. He said, "Julia, you don't know me, but can you meet with me and another minister this afternoon?" When we met they said, "We are district superintendents. We think you should know that the bishop told us in the cabinet to try to stop this 'Bolivia thing' that is getting 'out-of-hand.'"

I was shocked! I wept as I said to them, "I feel grief for him and for whatever it is that could motivate such action. But we couldn't stop it if we wanted to! It has been out of our hands for a long time."

Encumbered!

Other teams went to Bolivia. The bishop of the church there asked if we could provide a scholarship for the Bolivian who had been our team leader. Before we landed in Miami we had our strategy planned, and in just two months we had raised the funds for two years of study. Since I coordinated everything through the Latin American office in New York, I called to tell them the good news. They were furious!

The next year I took a team to Chile. The Latin American office graciously offered to send a letter of introduction commending us to the church of Chile. When I arrived there with a team of 16 volunteers, the district superintendent and the Board missionary showed me the letter. Attached to it was a personal note from the Latin American director saying, "Watch this woman. She does her own thing."

Again, it was grief I felt; not only because of the note, but because her relationship with that church was so poor that they would share her note with me-a relative stranger-out of their own grief and frustration.

The Volunteers In Mission program multiplied astronomically as a vital movement from the people in the pews across the Southeast. Soon I became a leader in VIM. For three years I served as dean of the United Methodist VIM Conference at Lake Junaluska, North Carolina. At the same time I was speaking all over the Southeast as a core interpreter for the Board of Global Ministries.

Whenever I met a mission board staff person on one of these trips, I would ask the troubling questions people were asking me, such as why there was so much difficulty in getting our funds to the field. None of my questions were ever answered.

In 1980 I was elected to serve on the conference Board of Missions. I was elected its president at the first meeting I attended. I was excited about this and said to myself, "Julia Williams the pew-sitter couldn't get answers, but Julia Williams the conference board president will. I'll have some clout. Our questions will be answered. Our funds will get to the field. Oh, Joy!" How wrong I was!

While all this was happening, I was speaking in churches across the jurisdiction and teaching in mission schools at Lake Junaluska. I was even invited to go to Kentucky to do several district spiritual life retreats for the UMW. I loved what God was calling me to do. My heritage had prepared me for it!

But as I worked as a conference officer, visiting churches and pastors and women across the church and hearing their concerns, I saw more problems and became more filled with grief. My telephone calls to New York were many. Conference calls with our treasurer and the treasurer's office in New York and letters, letters, letters-some signed by our entire board-were answered with one of two attitudes: We were either trouble-makers or were too dumb to understand the intricacies of the connectional system and the complexities of the international scene. They had too much to do to spend time answering their "critics."

Soon I began to ask myself, "What does this mean? I'm not dumb. Our North Carolina Board is not dumb. And many of us have spent more time on the international scene than those who are writing us those miserable responses. Is this what Christians who were nurtured in the church and are eager to serve are supposed to get from the offices which were created to enable us to be obedient to the Great Commission?"

Then one day I got a call from H. T. Maclin. I had known him for some time and had found him to be the only one who seemed to have really heard our concerns. H. T. had been the General Board's field representative for the Southeastern Jurisdiction. He told me how a group of United Methodists who loved their church-people who felt the same as I did-had formed a supplemental missions agency, The Mission Society for United Methodists. He asked me to serve on its board. I was ecstatic because I thought that now we would surely be able to get some issues resolved! I knew and respected many of the people who had organized the Mission Society. I knew that theirs were the finest mission-supporting churches in our denomination. Mostly, I felt hope!

And so I accepted H.T.'s invitation gladly, feeling that the North Carolina Conference could be a real reconciling agent. My conference board fully supported me. In fact, I was elected to the board for a second quadrennium with only three votes against me. But those three votes gave me insight into the next encumbrance. They came from the conference president of the United Methodist Women and the two women who happened to be sitting on either side of her.

A week after I accepted the Mission Society's invitation to be on its board and two weeks before the series of UMW spiritual life retreats were to begin in Kentucky, I received an early morning telephone call. The voice on the phone said to me, "I have never had to do anything so hard, but you are not to come to Kentucky. We are canceling the retreats. You have betrayed the United Methodist Church. We do not want to hear anything you have to say."

I said, "What did you say?" She repeated herself. I asked what was going on. She said they had been at the national UMW conference and found out I was on the board of that "other" agency. They had called New York to verify it and were told that I should not be allowed to speak.

I wept.

The next day a certified letter came saying, "Since you are a part of 'that' agency, we know you will not want to honor your commitment with us. Will you please send us a letter stating the same?"

It did not stop there. I went to Lake Junaluska where for 14 years I had attended Missions Week. That summer I taught on missions in the local church. There were 57 in my class, and we had a great time. Afterward the dean of the Missions Week came to ask me to teach again the next summer. "But you know," he said, "they called us and told us to take you off the program. We argued with

165

them and settled it by agreeing to put a monitor in your class." I called the office and asked, "Did you put a monitor in my class?" "Yes," was the reply.

I wept.

The journey continued. Each year we had more people at the Volunteers In Mission Conference. They were excited "pew people" doing the glorious work of witnessing. Their faith was growing, nurtured by those in all the countries where they went to serve, and they shared the stories here at home of what God was doing in their lives.

In 1985 I was scheduled to give the keynote address at the July VIM Rally and to teach missions once again. As had happened before, the Board in New York wrote and called asking that I be removed from the program. The program chairman refused-but that was the last year I was ever invited to do anything in the Southeast Jurisdiction in Volunteers-in-Mission.

The whole drama was like a horror story to me. It was so far removed from my heritage in a parsonage family in Louisiana and from the nurturing characteristics of the church I loved. Worst of all, I knew that if it was happening to me it must be happening to others as well all over the country.

I searched for answers with my pastor and my bishop; I made appointments, called my district superintendent and wrote letter after letter....

As a Core Interpreter for GBGM, I had known and respected H. T. Maclin. When he asked me to be on the board of the Mission Society and eventually to join the staff, I was thrilled. Now, I felt, I could finally lay aside every encumbrance and run the race! I remember the first Mission Society Board meeting I attended. I arrived late. As I walked into the room, Dr. L. D. Thomas, chairman of the board, got up from his chair and came to hug me and greet me. I thought, "There's an expression on his face like Daddy's." Then Ira Gallaway greeted me. I thought he, too, had that expression. As I looked around that room, and as I witnessed the board stopping to pray over and over again as hard issues were discussed, I felt the kind of peace and confidence you always get in the presence of godly people.

What I saw and felt at that meeting really was not complex. It was simple and right and good. And it was of God. It was what every person in every pew across our church hungers for: leaders with their eyes fixed on Jesus!

I had told my children when I left Raleigh to go to my first Mission Society meeting in Atlanta, "Mark this day on your calendar. I'm going to Atlanta to work with people who are part of a great movement of faith that will bring renewal to the church. We will be writing history." And history has proved that prediction to be true.

H. T. warned me that the opposition would be great. But I didn't know what an encumbrance was until I felt the grief and deep sadness we have experienced in our journey to restore the heritage of missions to our great church.

I learned in my journey just how serious is the battle for the soul of our great church.

I've learned in this journey that when God calls us to witness, He enables us to see the enemy clearly. He even gives us the courage to call sin, "sin," and the strength to lay aside its entangling, vicious hold.

We laypersons of the church feel it is time to "throw off everything that hinders and the sin that so easily entangles" (Hebrews 12:1) us in the United Methodist Church.

It is time for the leaders of the United Methodist Church to tell the staff of the Latin American office of the Board of Global Ministries to stop their concentrated attack on Bishop Roberto Diaz of Costa Rica and the blatant support and funding of those who would destroy the remarkable growth and development of the Evangelical Methodist Church of Costa Rica! It is time for the bishops of our church to reach out to this man who does with his life all we have talked about doing in this Convo.

At the 1989 Convo at Lake Junaluska, we began a network called the Evangelical Coalition for United Methodist Women to empower, educate and equip evangelical United Methodist women. We found out very quickly what the people in the pew think and believe-already more than 600 are in the network. The reaction from the Women's Division was swift also. One official sent a letter to all conference presidents across the nation telling them not to be a part of this "divisive group." The Women's Division stated that they are the only agency that may empower, equip and educate United Methodist women!

Recently I attended the UMW meeting in Kansas. The same kind of careful control was revealed in these statements from the leadership:

* 10,000 women were there for four days. There was not a single spontaneous prayer; everything was by rote (and they are supposed to be the "liberated" women.)
* The workshop on Central America was a constant attack on the United States; for example, the action in Panama was not because of Noriega's relationship with his people but to help Bush-it was "a 2 billion dollar drug bust."
* A joke was told by the leader - "Why has there never been a military coup in the U.S.? Because there is no U.S. Embassy in the U.S." (laughter) There were constant derogatory statements about the U.S.
* The mission books on Central America show a very limited view of what is happening in Latin America. They speak of liberation theology with no mention, except negatively, of the huge evangelical movement in all of Latin America.
* I found a new study book on the resource table. Written in March 1990 to supplement the study, it includes false information and another subtle attack on Roberto Diaz.

But as I wrote today's message and thought about what has happened in the years of the Mission Society-and of the renewal we have prayed for-I laughed out loud. Think of what we have already seen:

1. the birth of Bristol Books,
2. new Sunday school materials,
3. The Evangelical Coalition for United Methodist Women,
4. the Mission Society for United Methodists,

5. 77 new United Methodist missionaries sent out through the Mission Society for United Methodists, [Note: the total is far higher now in 1999]

6. the precious progress in the Dialogue,

7. the Committee on Evangelism in the Board of Global Ministries, and

8. the tremendous messages of the bishops at this Convo.

Renewal Is Happening!

I want to tell just one of my missionary stories. I just got bacGk from accompanying a team from Tanner-Williams United Methodist Church of Mobile to Costa Rica. I had spoken at their church several times. On my second visit, B.J. Sanderson came up to me and asked, "If we get up a work team, would you take us?" And I said, "Absolutely." Little did I know that in just a few months they were going to have assembled a good-sized team.

We went to Costa Rica last year with the first team, which included B. J., his wife Virginia and 14 others. B. J. recalls that after he suggested his idea, he began to think, "Well, you know, they're going to paint and build. Maybe I shouldn't go. Maybe I should just send my money." But a friend kept saying, "Now look, B. J., you need to go. Maybe you don't understand why God's asking you to go, but there's a reason. Have faith and go." B. J. finally decided to go to Costa Rica.

The first Sunday morning there we went to church. B. J. had a video camera, and he was recording everything on video. I saw him come down the side aisle and ask his wife for the Bible. He went to the back of the church and in a few minutes he motioned for me to come. B. J. was trembling. He said, "Julia, I prayed before I came here and asked God to reveal to me why I should come. I saw a vision of a little crippled child. Last night I had that same vision. Now I've come in here to this church and I want you to look on the back row. There is that child!" And he began to weep. He said, "What must I do? What must I do? I went to get the Bible and I opened it up and it said, '...anyone who has faith in me will do what I have been doing. He will do even greater things than these. . .'" (John 14:12). He said, "Julia, do you think God is telling me that the reason I came here is to enable him to heal that little child through me?" I looked at him and said, "Well, we certainly can't ignore what you are feeling."

I went up to tell the pastor. He stopped the service and called B. J. to the pulpit with me to translate, and B. J. told the story. The little child was brought to the altar. Many other people came up to that altar, and for 45 minutes we prayed for healing for all kinds of things that were brought to that altar. The preacher asked B. J. to lead the prayer.

After the service nobody wanted to go home. Everybody stayed around. There was something there that was so precious. A lady stood up and said, "I've got to tell you something. I didn't want to come to church this morning. I have been full of anger and awful thoughts for years. I want you to know I am free today!" I found out that day that this was the first time B.J. had ever prayed in public.

We went back to Costa Rica on a second work team just two weeks ago, and B. J. went again. We went back to that same church and the little girl came running up to B. J. and threw her arms around him. The mother told us that the child was scheduled for two operations, and the doctor said, "We don't have to do either one of them. She is well."

The laypersons of our church are trembling from encounters with God! - Permission to reprint given by Dr. Julia McLean Williams

Appendix N

Case Study: Ocracoke
United Methodist Church (OUMC)
Ocracoke Island, North Carolina

This discusses how a church addressed the problem of a pastor's attempting to implement her will against the wishes of the membership.

August 26th - October 29, 1994. On behalf of Concerned Methodists, I became involved in the events at Ocracoke United Methodist Church (OUMC). According to what I had learned from Mrs. Kathy O' Neal, a person who admitted to being lesbian was placed in position of working with the youth and was receiving the support of the pastor, who was Lisa Creech Bledsoe. The placement of the alleged lesbian was done over the objections of a majority of the congregation, but the pastor told the worship committee that she had the support of the District Superintendent, Bill Presnell, and Bishop C.P. Minnick. Some committee members walked out vowing to not return as long as the pastor was there. I advised Kathy, among other things, to tell people to not leave and for the people to not resign their positions. Reasons for this were: It's their church; some of the people had mortgaged their homes to be able to pay for the construction of the building 51 years ago; some of the people are third generation members of the church. The pastor dissolved the choir and told those who objected that if they didn't like her actions, they could leave and, "If everyone leaves the church and we have to close the doors, then so be it."

October 24, 1994. I met with 18 people on Ocracoke at Calvin O' Neal's house to talk about their problems. Wanting to get everyone's input, I started from the position of "Why am I here?" Then we worked chronologically up to the present time of Oct. 24th. According to the meeting, the people stated that:

* At an August 18th meeting of the worship committee, the worship committee stated who they wanted to have as choir director, and they wanted to minimize disruption. Lisa Bledsoe became angry and said, "I'm in charge. I make the decisions. You have nothing to do with it." The pastor then told the worship committee that Jolene Robinson had stated that she was a lesbian and was prepared to tell the youth the reasons for her lifestyle.

* When Kathy O' Neal tried to speak with the pastor about the problems, she told Kathy, "If you need time, it would be okay for you to step away from the church."

* The adult choir was disbanded by the pastor.

October 30, 1994. I attended the Charge Conference of their church, that was held during the regular church service. In the sermon, the DS who preached the sermon told the people that if they did not agree with the way things were going, they could leave the UMC. I saw the DS having the roll read so that only members of the Administrative Council could participate. The meeting saw people not members of the church and not on the Administrative Council but who were part of the pastor's "chosen few" vote on nominations and actions of the church. In addition, he refused to allow the whole congregation to vote, something that had not been done during the past fifty years, and ignored the objections of the people. I felt led to stand, ask to be recognized, identified myself, and suggested that perhaps he could allow all members to vote as had been done in the past. He stuck with his decision. Later when I asked to be recognized again, he yelled across the sanctuary, "No you will not be recognized. You are out of order! You just came out here to stir up trouble! You are not even a member of this congregation! I should bring charges against you!" Later, when he called on me to clear up a point, I emphasized that I had not gone out there to "stir up trouble" and that I had done nothing wrong. Afterwards, I went up to the DS, shook his hand, and reemphasized that the people had called me out of frustration not thinking they had anyone to whom they could turn. Then I talked to the pastor for about five minutes attempting to communicate to her the idea of ministry as serving the people's needs rather than trying to impose her will;

she was adamant in her position, so I left. Later, several members of the congregation commented on "how rude the DS was;" Lisa Caswell apologized to me for his conduct and wanted to go tell him that she thought he had been very rude. I told her that it was not necessary. Several of the people standing around asked, "Have you ever seen anything like that?" My response was: "Yes."

November 5, 1995. The date of a letter to "The Rev. William Presnell, District Superintendent, Elizabeth City District" that said:

"We, the undersigned members and friends of Ocracoke United Methodist Church, respectfully request you to convene a Church Conference at Ocracoke United Methodist Church.

At the charge conference on October 30, 1994 we feel the membership as a whole was not fairly represented. Although ignorance is no excuse, most of us did not realize that there was a difference between a Charge Conference and a Church Conference. In the past, these meetings have always been announced as Charge Conferences and the membership has been allowed to vote...You pointed out the problems we have had in the past. We feel that this congregation having input into the nominations and elections of its Board of Trustees and the Administrative Council is the only way we can move forward.

We apologize for any inconvenience this may cause you but we feel that this is absolutely necessary for our church to heal."
[Signed by 77 members and friends of the congregation of the OUMC.]

November 6, 1994. During the course of a subsequent conversation with Kathy, she was talking about the situation's being hopeless if the pastor has the support of the DS and the bishop. I advised her to ask to speak to the DS at some point in time and ask him if he knows that he has been asked to support the appointment of a lesbian to a position of leadership in the church, that he may not know it or that the pastor may have lied to them in saying that she had their support.

November 20, 1994. The date of a letter "To Whom it May Concern:"

"We, the undersigned members and friends of Ocracoke United Methodist Church, would like to clarify the fact that our Church has had problems for quite some time. These problems were not then and are not now due to Allen Morris as is being charged.

In a meeting with our District Superintendent in September he stated that the last three ministers 'were miserable' here at Ocracoke. This covers a span of 3 1/2 years. This fact should certainly clear up in your minds any doubts you may have about Mr. Morris 'stirring up trouble' out here on Ocracoke. Quite the contrary. Mr. Morris is the only one who has encouraged us to stay within the United Methodist Church. Mr. Morris was contacted in a desperate effort to find someone who could answer questions that were being raised here by members concerning Methodist policies.

When Mr. Morris was contacted, our minister had told a group of members in August that if they needed to leave the church then so be it. At our Charge Conference in October the District Superintendent told us if we weren't happy with the way things were run we needed to look for another church. (This is a little hard considering we live on a small island with access only by ferry and only one other church.)

People have left the church and no one within the Methodist Conference has reached out to them. Mr. Morris is the only person who has shown any concern over this situation. That is not stirring up trouble. That is what appears to be a genuine concern for the Methodist Church and its members. Allen Morris would have never been contacted had the 'powers that be' made some attempts to deal with the situation here on Ocracoke or even shown genuine concern for the members of this congregation."
[Signed by 27 members of the congregation of the Ocracoke church.]

November 23, 1994. I received the letter from the people at Ocracoke dated November the 20th containing the signatures of 27 people attesting to the fact that I had not caused disruption at their church. In this same mailing was a copy of a request for a

Church Conference (in which all members would be allowed to vote) signed by 77 members of the congregation of the Ocracoke church; this indicated widespread dissatisfaction with the October 30th conference, since normally only one conference is held per year and the average attendance at a Sunday service is 45 - 50.

November 30, 1994. Kathy O' Neal called and said that their people made a clean sweep of the elections and all of the pastor's supporters were removed from office. In accordance with my suggestion, she and a group of people met with the DS after the church conference and talked with him in private. They said that the pastor Lisa Creech Bledsoe needed to be moved because she was the problem; he agreed. She also told him that she resented Jimmy Creech's involvement in the affairs of their church (Lisa's dissolving the choir had been done when Creech was a pastor there before.). That was illegal. In response to my telling Mrs. O' Neal to ask him about his "support" of lesbianism in the church, he said that "he and Bishop Minnick did not know that Jolene was a lesbian and had not supported her being the youth choir director. The District Superintendent was apologetic to them for having lost his temper at the last meeting and stated that he had not truly understood the situation. She was effusive in the thanks she gave to Concerned Methodists and me.

October, 1994 - May, 1996. Believing that the pastor was damaging their church, and that they had not been helped by the denomination, OUMC members refused to pay the apportionments or her salary.

June 1995. Lisa Creech Bledsoe was reappointed away from OUMC.

March, 1996. I visited OUMC, met the current pastor, and was told at a luncheon "If it had not been for you (i.e., Concerned Methodists), we would not have a church today."

- Allen O. Morris, Concerned Methodists

Appendix O

Case Study: First United Methodist Church (FUMC)
Omaha, Nebraska

This case study discusses the turbulence caused in a church when their preacher Jimmy Creech performed a "same-sex" ceremony.

September 27, 1997. "Lesbian Ceremony Splits Methodist Congregation." 129 members of Creech's church mailed a letter to their fellow congregants stating their opposition to his actions. Among those signing were former U.S. Senator, Dave Karnes, his wife, Liz, and several other prominent and longtime members. The church has 1,900 members. The pastor called for a listening session with the two associate pastors, Rev. Don Bredthauer and Rev. Susan Mullins (both of whom support covenant ceremonies for homosexuals), as panelists. No one with opposing viewpoints has been asked to speak, Creech said, but they can air their views during a question and answer session. The group that sent out the letter called on members to sign the statement and to write [Bishop] Martinez. "We....must uphold the principles of our Christian faith that form the foundation of our beliefs and guide our lives," the groups said. "Any act to the contrary challenges these principles and cuts to the very essence of our being."
- Sources: The Omaha World Herald, by Julia McCord, Sept. 27, 1997; and United Methodist News Service (UMNS) release # 440

March 11-13, 1998. Jimmy Creech was found "not guilty" by a trial court that met in Kearney, Nebraska. Following the decision, Bishop Joel Martinez (Nebraska) lifted Creech's suspension and reaffirmed his appointment to First UMC, Omaha. A summary of the trial is as follows:

The trial court consisted of 13 clergymembers (8 men and 5 women) of the Nebraska Conference selected from a pool of

35...jurists. Following the decision, Creech told supporters, "...The great wall of bigotry [i.e., those opposing homosexuality] may not fall then [at General Conference 2000], but its collapse is inevitable, and we must be resolute at every stage and at every opportunity."

Witnesses for the Church called by Lauren Ekdahl, who served as counsel: 1. Jimmy Creech; 2. Bishop Kenneth W. Hicks (retired).

Witnesses for the Defense called by Doug Williamson, a religion professor at Nebraska Wesleyan University, [who was] Creech's counsel: 1. Glenn Loy, the clergyperson who brought charges against Creech; 2. Doug Bredthauer; 3 & 4. Joan Byerhof and Joanie Zetterman, former chairs of the staff parish relations committee; 5. Bill Jenks, current chair; 6. Jimmy Creech; 7. Roy Reed, a professor of worship at Methodist Theological School in Ohio; 8. Roy Black, a Black gay member of FUMC; 9. Phil Wogaman, pastor of Foundry UMC, Washington, D.C.; 10. Gregory N. Herek, research psychologist at the Univ. of California; 11. Betty Dorr, a member of FUMC.   - *Newscope, 3/20/98.*

[Observations: When it was discovered in February (before the trial began) that Lauren Ekdahl was to prosecute the case against Creech, Allen Morris called one of the laymen in Omaha who was pushing the case against Creech and told him that he (i.e., Morris) believed the stage was being set for Creech to be acquitted of the charges. Ekdahl was an officer in the Nebraska Methodist Federation for Social Action, which is extremely pro-active in promoting homosexual advocacy. After the trial, the report received from FUMC members present was that: evangelical pastors were systematically eliminated from the jury pool; there were few witnesses called by Ekdahl for the prosecution, with one being Creech himself; and the case presented for the "church's" side was weak. It is difficult to understand how the defense would have brought in a plethora of witnesses from as far away as Washington, D.C. and California, yet the prosecution neglected to call credible witnesses who were living in Omaha, were members of Creech's church, and were willing and available to testify. In the aftermath, Dr. Calvin Johnson, author of *Beyond the Point of No Return* stated, *"The*

178

Jimmy Creech case cannot be viewed as an isolated case that doesn't affect anyone else. If connectionalism does not apply here, then connectionalism is forever discredited."]

March 15, 1998. Jimmy Creech returned to the pulpit of FUMC where he received a standing ovation. [Note: The majority of members were absent, refusing to return to a church that Creech pastored; many of the people present were the homosexual population of Omaha.]

April 30, 1998. Date of letter from Mr. Robert L Howell to Bishop Sprague:

"Dear Bishop Sprague:

Although I am a lifelong Methodist and a fifty-four year member of First United Methodist Church of Omaha, I was not able to listen to your sermon last Sunday when you spoke in my church. Of the 1,900 members, I am one of the 1,700 that Jimmy Creech sacrificed in favor of 200. Seems unfair, doesn't it, to have someone steal your church because of their personal agenda?

Until fifteen months ago, I had been comfortable with the traditional teachings and beliefs of the Methodist Church and had confidence in the clergy. It probably serves no purpose at this time to tell you of Mr. Creech's disregard for The Bible and The Book of Discipline because he is merely the symbol of what is currently wrong with the United Methodist Church. While you are known to be in sympathy with the homosexual agenda, you must understand that the vast majority of members expect the Church to uphold the teachings of Jesus to love us even though we sin, but not accept our sins as being appropriate actions. I certainly would not want to be in the position of promoting sin as some within our denomination are doing.

With all due respect to your position, Bishop Sprague, I take exception to a recent comment attributed to you - that the homosexual issue 'is but one small issue' among those with which the church must deal. There has been no other issue since slavery that has caused such a deep division and threatens the future of the

179

Methodist Church. I further believe it short-sighted to oppose the spending of $1 million for a special session of the General Conference. Who could argue the good to be done in spending that money to feed children, etc. The Council of Bishops might, however, urge the spending of some of the stockpiled hundreds of millions of dollars for the many worthy causes for which members have been so generous. At the same time, using $1 million for a special session to save the Church seems appropriate so there will continue to be funds for such causes in the future. Only by getting the Church's affairs straightened out will there be members to continue providing monetary support.

I hope you had the time and interest last Sunday to discuss with Mr. Creech the attendance and income of FUMC, Omaha. Deep financial difficulties exist and, yet, they irresponsibly voted to undertake a major renovation project. I do not know how many attended on April 26 to listen to you, but would suspect that there were more than the approximately 200 persons normally attending all three services. I worshiped in a school auditorium with over 300 in one service. That is a strong message of the faith people still have after being disenfranchised by their pastor.

Our prayers are with you and your peers, Bishop Sprague, as you engage in discussions in Lincoln that could very well be the making or the breaking of the United Methodist Church.

- Robert L. Howell"

June, 1998. Jimmy Creech was not reappointed as the senior pastor of FUMC, Omaha. Doug Bredthauer, who is supportive of Creech's same-sex covenanting ceremonies, was.

- Source: Lay member of FUMC, Omaha

June 16, 1998. Letter from Diane West, member of FUMC, Omaha.

"Hello,

I'm not quite sure why I'm going to tell all of you about this, but I would guess it's because it helps me to deal with it.

Tonight, several of us in the Laity Group at FUMC Omaha attended a Church Council meeting at FUMC. There wasn't any huge *reason for it other than we have been trying to attend these meetings. I knew in my heart, while I was sitting there, that I would probably never be back in that building again. I know that I cannot return to church life there now or anytime in the foreseeable future. I am just speaking for myself, not for anyone else in the Laity Group.*

Anyway, all the good memories I had of being a part of the church in that building ran through my mind. They were all as clear as day.. kind of like the picture I have in my mind of my grandfather. The night he died, we had been over to his house to visit. As I was standing on the porch saying good-bye, something told me to turn around one more time and take a good look at his face so that I would always remember what he looked like. I will always remember my grandfather's face under that porch light.

At church tonight, I saw all kinds of warm, wonderful pictures in my mind. I saw myself as a little girl running down the steps from Sunday school class with my papers in my hand, playing Red Rover on the lawn, trying to remember the words to the songs for the Christmas program, sitting in the balcony on Christmas Eve with my family and hearing the pipe organ, having snacks in the huge kitchen (which I always thought was really cool)...all the way through seeing my wedding day and other events in recent years. I won't bore you with all the details.

After that, I decided that I needed a break from the meeting. So, while everyone else was still sitting there, I slipped out the door and walked around the building all by myself. I looked at all the rooms with so many memories one last time. I wasn't sure if I really wanted to see the Sanctuary, but I decided I would head that way. I got as close to it as I could. It was dark and really quiet. I tried to open the door to look inside, but it was sealed shut. There was a big sign on the door that said, "Hard Hat Area." I stared at it for a long time. Finally, I just said "Good-bye" and turned around and went back down the hallway.

I know the church is just a building, but it holds a lot of memories. I was very thankful that God had imprinted so many nice memories in my mind and that He gave me a chance to say goodbye. It makes the death a little less difficult to bear.

I apologize for boring you with my little story...I guess it just turned out to be a bit more painful than I thought it would.

Please keep us in your prayers as we have our big meeting tomorrow night about the direction our group will take. I also came to terms tonight with the fact that whatever happens may not be what I wish could happen. I asked God with all my heart to please make sure that whatever decision is made will be His will. I know it will be because I know He heard me.

Diane"

- Source: E-Mail from Diane West, member of "FUMC"; June 16, 1998

June 5, 1999. Creech will continue to defy church law. Jimmy Creech, who was tried by the UMC for performing a lesbian marriage, said... [that] he will continue to defy church law and perform such ceremonies.

- Lincoln Journal Star, Lincoln, Nebraska

Appendix P

Case Study: Salem United Methodist Church
Lodi, California

Following is a case study involving Salem United Methodist Church [SUMC] in the California-Nevada Conference. In this situation, 27 members of the church, leaders who served on key boards, were removed from the church without their prior knowledge. They were asking that they receive a pastor who reflected their views. The complete timeline is available on the Concerned Methodists' website on the internet.

January 1997. Letter presented to the DS, by the PPRC at the January meeting outlining the PPRC's thoughts as to the theology of the church and as to what was needed in a pastor selected for them.

"Of our last six pastors (one served for about 6 months) five of them were in the last years of their service with between 3-5 years before their retirement. Some of them were liberal in their theology and we lost many family groups due to that." - Sincerely, Salem PPRC

[Comment from our contact: *"The chairperson of our PPRC was in contact with the DS from time to time for several weeks and months."*]

May 13, 1997. A letter was sent out to all members of the congregation to include the pastor. It said in part: *"For the past three months, your Pastor-Parish Committee [PPR] has been in negotiations with the Methodist Conference via our D.S. Through negotiations, we have been...trying to find what the conference calls 'a good church/pastor [m]atch'. With regret, these negotiations have netted poor results....   Dear friends, in talking with many of you, seeing many in our family of believers leaving our fellowship,* *and finances being drained, the Pastor-Parish Committee saw this as our last and only hope for Salem's future. However, Salem's request was turned down....You are invited to a meeting for the entire congregation on Sunday, May 18, at 4:30 p.m. [at Reese School]...to discuss where we have been, what has transpired between the Methodist Conference and SUMC's PPR..., and what the future may hold for each of us in regard to where we are now..*

Sincerely,

[The names of the PPRC Chair and the Finance Committee Chair appeared with the names of twenty-five other people.]

May 18, 1997. A statement read by Pastor Steven Darling after worship on Sunday contained in part: "I have sent a copy of this letter [dated May 13, 1997 to our D.S., Dave Bennett, who has conferred with our Bishop, Melvin Talbert and other members of the cabinet."

May 19, 1997. An "Announcement of a church conference to elect new officers" was not sent to the individual who had supplied the information on the Lodi church and who was one of the persons removed from membership. This announcement said, in part, "To be elected: Church Council Chair, Treasurer, Saff-Parish Relations Chair and members, Lay Member to Annual Conference, [and to] Receive Report of Membership as of this date..."

May 19, 1997. The date of a letter received from the pastor of Salem church, Steve Darling, to one of the persons removed. It said in part, "...it is my responsibility to acknowledge that you are removed from the rolls of Salem United Methodist Church according to paragraph 243, page 136 of *The Book of Discipline, 1996* and accordingly, from the offices you hold in the congregation." [Note: Paragraph 243 states that "Persons may be removed from the roll of baptized members by death, transfer, withdrawal or removal for cause." This paragraph is followed by #244 which further states "Persons may be removed from the roll of professing members by death, transfer, withdrawal, charge conference action or removal for cause (See pars. 229, 231, 236-243, 2627.4)" Par.

2627.4 starting on page 670 of The Book of Discipline, 1996 entitled "Trial of Lay Member of a Local Church...."]

May 20, 1997. Letter sent to the members of SUMC, except those names who were on the list of the earlier letter and considered to still be members: "As of yesterday we have noted the withdrawal of the 27 persons from our official rolls and they have been requested to relinquish to the office their records, monies, bank books or whatever they have of Salem UM's property."
- Grace & Peace, Pastor Steve

May 22,1997. Date of a follow-up letter to the meeting held at Reese School on May 18. We [in Concerned Methodists] have been told that as of this time the 27 persons whose names appeared at the bottom of the May 13th letter had not received their letters of removal.

May 28, 1997. Date of the Salem Church Conference chaired by the DS and attended by the Fresno DS. A letter was presented to the Salem Church Conference during the meeting by one of the persons who had been removed from membership, who also requested during the meeting to be given the reason for "removal for cause". The letter said in part:

"In a letter dated May 20, 1997, mailed out to the Salem Church membership from Steven Darling, pastor of Salem Church [that] said, and I quote, "As of yesterday we have noted the withdrawal of the 27 persons from our official rolls.." This statement is incorrect and not true. Not one of the 27 members sent in a letter asking to be removed from membership, nor did any of them ask to be removed from membership as of the above stated date. What has taken place is that this conference, the conference to which each of you belong has taken it upon themselves to remove the 27 members from the rolls of Salem United Methodist Church. This was done on their part, as they say, according to Paragraph 243, page 136 of *The Book of Discipline, 1996*, which says, quote, 'Persons may be removed from the roll of baptized members by death, transfer, withdrawal or removal for cause, with the understanding that withdrawal or removal for cause in no way abrogates the baptismal covenant from God's side.' Unquote.

I wish it to be made know to this Charge and the members of [SUMC] that I did not die, I did not transfer, I did not submit any form of resignation for withdrawal. That only leaves 'removal for cause.'"

August 6, 1997. Date of letter received with the explanation for 'removal for cause' from the Delta D.S., said in part: "Grace and Peace to you in the name of our Lord Jesus Christ....It is clear from the statements made in the [original] letter and from the intention of the May 18, 1997, meeting that those who signed the letter, by their own words were no longer supporting the United Methodist Church. Thus, these statements are the basis for "removal for cause" of these persons' names from the membership rolls of Salem United Methodist Church of Lodi." Grace and Peace, David L. Bennett

August 16, 1997. Statement from a former member of SUMC of Lodi: "The thing I found most interesting was that there was no attempt to call PPRC, back into conference to see if any reconciliation was possible."

Observation: It is curious that these members, leaders in Salem UMC, would have been removed from membership for striving to get a pastor supportive of their church's orthodox Christian beliefs, yet no significant action has been taken against those who have performed "same-sex" ceremonies (which the authority in that conference has openly supported).

Appendix Q

Case Study: St. Francis United Methodist Church (SFUMC)
San Francisco, California

Following is a timeline of the history of SFUMC in the California - Nevada Conference, the effort to keep its church open and to prevent the facilities that they estimate to be valued at approximately $1,000,000, from being seized by the conference. While we in Concerned Methodists do not agree with all of the actions taken by the members, we understand the personal agonies they have felt and the reasons for their actions. A more complete timeline is available on the Concerned Methodists website.

1946. SFUMC starts as a house church.

1955. SFUMC incorporates, having built a one-story church; it purchases the house and property next door for a parsonage.

1972. SFUMC entered a ministry agreement with Presbyterian Church.

1995. In disagreement over the direction of church outreach, SFUMC voted to end the joint ministry with the Presbyterian Church.

January 1996. District Superintendent (DS) C. Cordes introduced a motion at annual church meeting to close SFUMC. The motion was defeated. Bishop Melvin Talbert appointed a quarter-time pastor, who was instructed by the DS to not encourage the congregation, since SFUMC could be closed at the upcoming June 1996 Annual Conference meeting. The congregation commenced outreach to community, and developed a children's ministry.

May 13, 1996. Letter from DS Cordes to Dr. Frank Leeds, Administrative Board Chair, that the decision had been made to recommend that SFUMC be discontinued as of July 1, 1996.

June, 1996. DS Cordes' motion at Annual Conference to close SFUMC was tabled. Bishop Talbert called for a second vote: that vote was the same as the first, to table the motion, giving SFUMC a victory.

July, 1997. Bishop Talbert appointed Rev. Charles Lerrigo half time to SFUMC. He did not participate in church weekday programs and invited intoxicated persons to church services, causing the church to reek. He began to unilaterally adjourn Administrative Council meetings. Sunday worship declined; programs collapsed; and giving declined. Pastor Lerrigo tape recorded church meetings over church members' objections.

March, 1998. Evangelical pastors and laypersons, meeting at Oakdale United Methodist Church, published the "Oakdale Declaration," asking for separate Evangelical Conference.

March 14, 1998. Pastor Capuli was quoted in the *San Francisco Examiner* that he would, if given the opportunity, perform rituals of holy union between same sex partners. (Src.: Paper furnished by SFUMC members)

April, 1998. Over the opposition of Rev. Lerrigo, the SFUMC Ad. Council endorsed the Oakdale Declaration, the only church in the Golden Gate District to do so.

May, 1998. The PPRC of SFUMC rejected the appointment of Rev. Capuli as pastor of their church.

May, 1998. DS Thomas Kimball announced the appointment of Rev. Arturo Capuli, full time pastor of a nearby ethnic church, Grace UMC. Rev. Capuli, who in exchange for a monthly salary of $1,000, was to give two sermons a month at SFUMC, was also to attend SFUMC meetings.

June, 1998. At a special church meeting called to approve Rev. Capuli's compensation package, the entire congregation except one walked out after he refused to table the motion. The one member voted "no" to the package.

July, 1998. Rev. Lerrigo retired from the active ministry and subsequently co-officiated with more than 70 other UM clergy at a ceremony for two women, one of whom is the Cal-Nevada Lay Leader.

September, 1998. Rev. Capuli began taking members from Grace to St. Francis, making them members of SFUMC for the stated reason that those persons wished to attend SFUMC's earlier worship service. Grace members Minda Doctolero, cousin of Pastor Capuli, and Julius and Phoebe Abundo, transferred their memberships to SFUMC in August.

September - October, 1998. In response to the flood of members from Grace, SFUMC members leafleted Grace, asking the congregation to not support Rev. Capuli's plan to use members of Grace to out-vote SFUMC members at the next SFUMC conference. The SFUMC Administrative Council voted to cease paying apportionments, and continued to refuse to pay Rev. Capuli. SFUMC members begin picketing Grace Sunday mornings. One screamed at Mrs. Evelyn Fernandez-Jones, "Why don't you just conform?"

December 13, 1998. At the SFUMC annual church meeting presided over by DS Kimball, members from Grace voted to oust SFUMC's church leadership. Rev. Kimball overruled all objections to the fact that members from Grace were voting, and disregarded church corporation by-laws. Rev. Capuli announced he would admit no more members to SFUMC unless such persons first attend a 13-week preparatory class, which he will announce in the future. SFUMC members continued to picket Grace.

Late December, 1998. In a series of meetings, outgoing SFUMC leadership spent down almost the entire church treasury by advance paying bills, etc. Rev. Capuli unsuccessfully attempted to cancel meetings.

January, 1999. SFUMC members formed a house church, meeting on   Saturday evenings. Almost the entire SFUMC congregation ceased attending Sunday morning services at SFUMC.

February, 1999. Rev. Capuli announced that Sunday mornings would be discontinued at St. Francis for the convenience of those attending.

February 13, 1999. The wife of DS Kimball, Connis Kimball, knocked down Evelyn Fernandez-Jones (who sustained a broken wrist) the wife of John Jones, who was picketing in front of the district parsonage on a public sidewalk. Mrs. Kimball stood over Mrs. Fernandez-Jones yelling and threatening to hit her again. John Jones responded by running into Mrs. Kimball, knocking her backward onto the ground. She was also injured.

March 3, 1999. Bishop Talbert denied the appeal of conduct of the December 13, 1998 election, and accepted DS Kimbal's assurances that the membership list was accurate and only church members voted.

March 14, 1999. A special charge conference was held at SFUMC that removed John Jones from his church office; it was called after Pastor Capuli and the DS had secured a temporary restraining order preventing John Jones from going closer than 50 yards to the St. Francis church building.

June 4, 1999. A special St. Francis Charge Conference, held at the home of DS Kimball, approved the merger of St. Francis into Grace.

August 7, 1999 - Present. SFUMC house church, now calling itself a "church in exile," continues to meet on Saturday evenings.

Appendix R

Case Study: First United Methodist Church
Kingsburg, California

Following is a case study involving First United Methodist Church, Kingsburg (FUMC-K) in the California-Nevada Conference as it became the independent Kingsburg Community Church (KCC).

June 29, 1998. Kingsburg Methodists split from denomination: Lowell and Lois Johnson celebrated the 50th anniversary of their marriage at FUMC-K here by resigning Sunday from the denomination, along with 198 other church members. "It's exciting. It's a good thing. We've seen this coming," Lowell Johnson said. "We have two separate faiths in this denomination that cannot be held together," the Rev. Ed Ezaki said in his sermon preceding the vote. Ezaki and other lay leaders said that current Methodism has forsaken the Bible by allowing same-sex marriages, encouraging sexual permissiveness, questioning the lordship of Jesus Christ and failing to include conservatives in top church positions. "There are some things in life that require absolute purity, and following God is one of them," he said. The vote was 200 to 0 in favor of leaving the denomination, and also launched KCC.. Among those who did not resign were Ezaki and the church's board of trustees, because they will now try to negotiate purchase of church properties from the denomination. A key player in that effort will be the Rev. Rick Plain, the Methodist superintendent who oversees the 62 churches of the Fresno District. Speakers and others at the service expressed sadness, eagerness to take what, in the truest sense, is a leap of faith. "We've got to go forward with our children," said Chrisann Boone, Christian education director. She's now worrying whether she'll have a building to house vacation Bible school. "If we lose this building, that's a sacrifice I'm willing to pay because I'm not willing to waver on my core values," Scott Carlson said.

In a comment to *The Fresno Bee* newspaper, Ezaki said "100 percent" of Kingsburg's 371 members are planning to leave. During the vote, dozens of people from other Kingsburg churches stood outside, holding hands in prayer circles as a show of support. Among them was Kingsburg Mayor John A. Wright. "We're working with the healing process," said Wright, a Mennonite Brethren.
- E-mail from Janz Mynderup; original source is believed to be UMNS.

July 7, 1998. *California congregation leaves denomination.*
SAN FRANCISCO (UMNS) — About 200 members of the Kingsburg (Calif.) United Methodist Church declared that "in Christian conscience" they could no longer remain members of the denomination. They transferred their membership to a newly created KCC effective July 1. Expressing regret that the congregation came to the point of leaving, Bishop Melvin G. Talbert said, "My prayers go with them." Fresno District Superintendent Richard Plain said he would begin the process, spelled out in the denomination's *Book of Discipline*, to explore the possible discontinuance of the church...The disciplinary process is an involved consultation that could take months. This is not the first time UMs in the conference have broken with the denomination. Last year, a number of members left Salem UMC in Lodi, Calif. A partial walk-out is also occurring in Oakdale [pastored by The Rev. Kevin Clancey].

Both Ezaki and Clancey have been leaders in the California-Nevada Evangelical Renewal Fellowship (ERF), which in April asked church leaders to create a separate conference for evangelicals.
- UMNS #396; July 7, 1998; Nashville, Tenn.; 10-21-28-71B{396}.

July 16, 1998. Cal/Nev Conference Breaks Trust - All Assets Seized
On Wednesday, July 16th, the Conference Treasurer seized approximately $14,000 in cash left in the KUMC checking account.... about 19 checks were outstanding and most have bounced including the payroll check for the pastor Rev. Ed Ezaki, the secretary's accrued vacation pay, and the payroll tax deposit. Approximately

three hours before the pastor was informed, he and the Conference Treasurer had discussed the importance of acting honorably in order to produce a win-win situation and avoid an emotional overreaction on either side. Thursday evening, the Conf. Board of Trustees are going to Kingsburg to meet with the former KUMC Trustees, and are asking for immediate relinquishment of the deeds for property (they're bringing a notary), the personal property, and dissolution of the KUMC corporation. The pastor Ed Ezaki and the trustees will be consulting legal counsel in order to determine the next steps. The pastor observed, "The larger question is: how much can you trust people who have just lied to you? Now that I've had a couple of days of pain and anger, I can see that even these dishonorable and immoral actions serve the cause of Christ. They will take everything from any church that has the moral courage to oppose them. And for them, the end justifies the means." - Source: E-mail from conference member; July 22, 1998

July 22, 1998. World Magazine has an article about the Kingsburg Church...The conference plans to take the property evidently and evict the congregation. Pray for them.
- E-mail; Bob Kuyper, Editor, Transforming Congregations. The information was available at http://www.worldmag.com/world/home.asp

July 22, 1998. So Much for Good Faith and Eye Ball to Eye Ball Truths.

"Above reproach, the bible indicates its overseers are to be. Reflecting back on dealings in the UMC at local and conference levels, I can recall incidents where "just turn the other way" on matters and it will be OK or "we don't have to answer that..." and a list of this type of verbal and psychological abuse will run a rather long gambit. But that is just one of many issues of this alerting note:

Kingsburg UMC has ceased to be an entity with its bank account seized - approximately $14,000 dollars - and other assets frozen after a meeting where those in "power" were working together so all would have a "win-win" results, a person in the "know"

has reported. Rev Ed Ezaki's UMC ordination orders have been surrendered, July 15th, 1998 as well....Now that is real top-notch UMC leadership. So much for trust! So much for conference, district and DS words of affirmation to a pastor and the flock."
- Source: E-mail from Janz I. Mynderup, who has served with the California-Nevada Conference; Saturday, July 18 1998

July 24, 1998. "KUMC trustees and KCC Directors met last night with two Conference trustees, the Conference Treasurer and The DS Rick Plain. It began as a tense encounter. We asked for explanation of the deceptive manner in which KUMC funds had been seized last week. All we got was evasion and blame-passing. All I heard was the Nuremberg defense: we were just following orders. It came out that the DS had indeed been primed to declare the church abandoned last week. He didn't even tell the District Board of Church Location and Building. We were set up. I will pray that the DS grows some integrity through this process. Nonetheless, the good news is that we were able to move from the details to talk about the big issue. That is, we agreed that there was an unknown sum of money that will make the whole issue go away. It was clear that if we could agree on the price, the conference trustees were ready to clear the whole thing up last night. They are, looking to make enough money on the deal to make it seem to the Annual Conference that they "won." I feel that the KCC Board Chair was right when he observed that the Conference does not want to give us any credit for moral ownership of any of the property. I do not know if we will be able to find agreement when we feel that 80 years' of building, paying for and caring for the buildings makes them ours regardless of the Discipline and they feel that the buildings were built for the Annual Conference.

I pointed out to the trustees that the UMC has a long history of supporting land reform in Central and South America. The UMC has taken the position that generations of working the land and living on it gives peasants a moral claim on it regardless of the legal title held by the rich absentee landowners. In my opinion, the situation we are in is analogous. The family of faith in Kingsburg built these buildings. I have a 71 year old grandmother in the church whose grandfather scraped out the basement with his mule team and a scraper. Her mother came across the street from school every day to nail lath to the beams before the plasterers went to work. Over the past 7 years that I have been in Kingsburg, we have spent $500,000 on improvements, carpet, air conditioning, structural repair and the like. The Conference has never spent a dime on the buildings in Kingsburg. Yet, they believe that they own them. The land belongs to the peasants.

I repeat my previous observation that if we didn't have sufficient reason to leave the UMC before, we sure understand why we left now. How could we have remained a part of something so immoral for so long? How could we have supported it with our membership and our apportionment dollars? Pastor GL Johnson of People's Church in Fresno, the largest church in these parts with about 3,000 on Sunday morning, preached last Sunday mentioning our struggle and commending me by name. He also pledged that if we had to buy our buildings, he would take up a collection. Other churches in town have pledged fund raisers and bake sales to help us buy the buildings. To me that is the heart of God for the true Body of Christ. There is no legal obligation for a former Assembly of God church to help out a little country church in Kingsburg, but GL and those like him see it as being faithful to a higher trust, being faithful to God. In Him, Ed Ezaki"
Source: E-mail, Ed Ezaki;Friday, July 24, 1998 8:25 AM

May 14, 1999. Greeting from KCC. Ed Ezaki wrote:
"Well, the day of freedom has finally arrived! Yesterday afternoon May 13th, title to our buildings was recorded in our name with Fresno County and escrow closed with the Methodist Conference. Thanks for your support and prayers through a difficult year of waiting. The grand total purchase price was $227,562.53 to the Annual Conference. We get the buildings and contents, the parsonage subject to the remaining mortgage, and half of the $20,125 bank account. It looks like we have about $100,000 to raise to pay the whole thing off by year end (our goal). Praise the Lord for His deliverance. What a great relief it is to feel like I no longer have to watch every word, fearing reprisals from the Annual Conference.

Things continue to grow; we will receive 32 new members on June 23rd (including the 9 fearless ones who remained UMC trustees of the shell of KUMC, soon going out of business). We continue to pray for those who remain a biblical witness within the UMC. However, I humbly offer my service and experience to any who are exploring following our path. As I like to tell my students when I teach Revelation, "Good news. If you skip to the end, God wins! - Blessings," Ed Ezaki - Source: E-mail; Fri. May 14 17:02:42 1999.

August 18, 1999. We have received a report that $50,000 from the FUMC-K settlement will be put into a fund by the California-Nevada Conference for legal fees to pay for pursuing future claims against the property of local churches.
     - E-mail received from layman in the Cal.-Nevada Conference

Appendix - S

Case Study: First United Methodist Church (FUMC-M)
Marietta, Georgia

Prior to the events in this case study, Dr. Charles Sineath apologized to the FUMC-M Administrative Board for withholding information from them. The laity leadership in the church then formed a study team (coincidentally, composed mostly of ladies from the church) to examine serious areas in the denomination - and the role that The First United Methodist Church of Marietta (FUMC-M) had in supporting them. This case study has a letter of explanation from Dr. Charles Sineath and continues with a letter of explanation by the members of the committee; a narrative of subsequent actions; and the outcome. The complete text of the letter from Charles Sineath ("A") and the Introduction ("B") along with all of the references used for the redirection of that part of their apportionment may be found at website: http://www.atlantagolfer.com/fumc/

A. Cover Letter from Charles Sineath, [pastor of] First United Methodist Church - Marietta, Georgia:

"The material in this report is not meant to be an indictment of The United Methodist Church. Rather, it is an attempt to tell the truth about things we believe must be known if our denomination is to continue to make a strong and transforming witness to the world, be found faithful to our Wesleyan heritage, and our Biblical, orthodox theological roots. This report points out problems within our denomination that strike at the heart of our faith, and are a serious threat to the integrity of the church that you and I love. The issues addressed here are scriptural and theological. Persons in strategic places and positions in our denomination have challenged the basic tenets of our Christian faith: the incarnation, denying that Jesus Christ is God in human flesh, fully divine as well as fully human; denying the atoning efficacy of Christ's death on the Cross; denying the reality of His bodily resurrection as a seal of our redemption; denying the authority of Scripture as the Word of God, containing all things necessary for salvation, faith and practice.

This report has been prepared because we love The United Methodist Church, and are fully aware of all the ways it has, and continues even now to please and honor God. The focus is not meant to condemn, but to redeem and restore. A beloved brother in Christ recently learned that he had cancer of the prostate. Obviously this malignancy became an area of focus in his life. Imagine if I had said to him, "John, why are you focusing on that prostate that is malignant? After all, your eyes are healthy, your hearing is good, your hair is in good shape, your teeth are sound, your arms and legs and liver and heart are all in good shape. With so much that is good, why don't you focus on that instead of focusing on your prostate? After all, it's small, and nobody can even see it!" Obviously, that would be ridiculous. The reason he is focusing on the area that is cancerous is not because it's big, and not because he's unaware of the health of the rest of his body. He's focusing on the cancer because he knows that if he doesn't, it will someday kill him!

In the second chapter of Revelation we find Jesus' letter to the church at Thyatira (verses 18-28). Our lord affirms the overall goodness of the church there (v.19): "I know your deeds, your love and faith, your service and perseverance, and that you are now doing more than you did at first. (v.20) Nevertheless, I have this against you; you tolerate that woman Jezebel..." That's my feeling about The United Methodist Church today. I know, and I hope you know, that the Lord knows our multitude of good deeds, our continuing love and faith, our ongoing service and perseverance, that we United Methodist Christians are doing more good than ever before. That's not in question. No doubt about it. The problem is that we are tolerating things that Jesus says are intolerable, that strike at the very root of our faith.

Friends, we must not tolerate that which our Savior says is intolerable, that which contradicts Holy Scripture, that which violates the Doctrinal integrity of our church. We must not, and God willing we will not! I believe God wants to preserve The United Methodist Church as a purified Bride of Christ. And I believe God wants to use us as one of His instruments in doing that."

- Charles Sineath

B. The reasons for withholding that part of the apportionment, as formulated by the study committee by FUMC-M:

"Over the past two hundred years, the contributions of the United Methodist Church to the United States and the world cannot be overestimated. During the 20th century, the United Methodist Church has been a vital force in meeting the needs of the oppressed, the poor, and the sick around the world. Significant contributions to Christian spiritual growth within the denomination have occurred through programs such as Disciple Bible Study and Walk to Emmaus. Local United Methodist churches have been vital places for equipping the body, fellowship, and care and comfort. These kinds of positive contributions are not in dispute.

The issue before us is rather the doctrinal integrity of the United Methodist Church: the faithfulness of its leadership to adhere to our Doctrinal Standards and to champion the cause of Jesus Christ as the Son, Savior, and Lord. In a relativistic and secular society, the responsibility of the church is to uphold the basic, foundational tenets of the Christian faith. Therefore, we must determine if the United Methodist Denomination has fulfilled this duty and responsibility.

A very important point to be made in understanding this crisis is that as a denomination we have strong Christian doctrinal standards. These have changed very little since John Wesley wrote them in 1784 and none at all since 1808 when a restrictive rule went into effect preventing any changes to these doctrinal standards. If we are faithfully following those doctrinal standards, there will be no question but that we are contending "for the faith that was once for all entrusted to the saints" Jude 1:3 (NIV)

The report that follows gives evidence of individual factual incidents. The crisis in the UMC is serious and long-standing but for the most part the report focuses on the last ten to twenty years. As the report is read, it should be kept in mind that these individual actions are simply indicative of much larger problems. To assist in putting these individual incidents in perspective, we will identify several overall trends or patterns in the United Methodist Church.

First, United Methodist seminaries are no longer strictly adhering to the basic doctrines of the Christian faith and are tolerating if not promoting some non-Christian theologies. Radical feminist theology is one of the more visible of those. The basic tenets of radical feminist theology include rejection of the Bible as an authoritative document because of its "patriarchialism", identification of the crucifixion of Jesus Christ as "divine child abuse" that has no relevance for modern women, and promotion of worship of pagan female deities. The report may seem to include a disproportionate number of references to women, but it is because of the pervasive influence that radical feminist theology has had on United Methodism.

The hold that feminist theology has on UM seminaries cannot be underestimated. For example, one of the foremost proponents of feminist theology, Rosemary Radford Ruether, is a tenured professor at Garrett-Evangelical Theological Seminary and Aida lsasi-Diaz another well-known feminist/liberationist theologian, is on the staff at Drew University Seminary. The Re-Imagining Conference of 1993 (which was characterized by worship of the goddess Sophia and denial of the person and work of Jesus Christ) was not an isolated event. It has been repeated three more times since then and the keynote speakers are always Protestant and Catholic seminary professors or clergy.

Second, from the very highest levels of leadership on down, many UM bishops, clergy and staff; most of whom have graduated from UM seminaries, have exhibited a reluctance to adhere to the basic doctrines of the Christian faith. The emphasis on a diverse, inclusive social gospel has eclipsed the need to preach "Jesus Christ and Him crucified." Intellectualism has snuffed out a simple faith in Bible as the primary means through which the Creator has sought to reveal Himself to man. This lack of adherence to the essential doctrines of the Christian faith is evident in many of the incidents included in the report.

Third, the staffs of the general hoards and agencies have become so isolated from the laity that they act with almost no regard for the beliefs or wishes of the majority of church members. The examples of liberal political activism in this report are typical of the pattern of behavior exhibited by these staff members.

Finally, all efforts at renewal by organized clergy and laity have failed to elicit significant improvement in these problems. The failure to discipline clergy who have been guilty of violating the doctrinal standards of the church is strong evidence of the disdain of the church leadership for the concerns being expressed by the church membership."

C. MEMO: Board of Marietta First United Methodist Votes to Direct Apportionments

Date: March 22, 1998
To: Board of Stewards
From: Select Committee
Regarding: Conference Apportionments

We have looked closely at our Conference Apportionments and are submitting the following recommendations. Please be aware that our total Conference Apportionments are $235,985. However, we have already sent in our total for the Atlanta Marietta District Work Fund of $12,579. That leaves $223,406.

We recommend that we direct this entire amount, $223,406, on a line item basis in order to support only those official United Methodist ministries beyond our local church (and primarily within the bounds of our North Georgia Conference and Southeastern Jurisdictional Conference) that we are convinced honor God, are pleasing to Him, are scripturally sound, and are in keeping with our Vision as a local United Methodist Church. By such action we enhance our prophetic witness to and within the church and denomination as good stewards of the funds entrusted to us. By directing these funds on a line item basis we insure that they will be used to underwrite only the ministries we designate, and will not be used in any way to support ministries we do not wish to underwrite.

We recommend the following ministry investments:

Episcopal Residence Fund	210.75
District Superintendents Fund	16,129.51
Equitable Compensation Fund	3,161.32
Board of Ordained Ministry	1,183.24
Underpayment Factor	2,738.11
Retired Ministers Conference Insurance	16,644.09
Retired Past Service Pension	21,163.91
Jurisdictional Administration	1,545.73
Annual Conference Expenses	2,816.06
Council on Finance and Administration	6,913.93
Office of Ministerial Service	3,352.68
Office of Church Developmen	2,178.04
Annual Conference Council on Ministries	22,169.44
Urban Action	8,442.32
Homeless Council	745.98
Hispanic Ministries	703.47
Conference Task Forces	537.72
Mission Initiatives	656.29
Jurisdictional Mission Fund	2,262.33
Simpsonwood	162.95
Black College Fund	5,805.00
Africa University	1,346.00
Capital Funding	1,757.00
Christian Higher Educ/Campus Ministry	14,695.00
Church Development	27,618.00
Total	$164,938.87

This leaves a remainder of $58,427.13 which we recommend be directed to the following three United Methodist Ministries that clearly meet the criteria listed above, and are in special need at this time:

* Building Program, Wesley Foundation University of Georgia - $25,000.00
* Camp Glisson Redevelopment Project - $25,000.00
* Mountain Top Boys Home - $8,427.13

Please take note that the amounts [of Conference Apportionments] we are recommending are exactly as the amounts requested except for the five line items that are omitted altogether. These are in areas where we have doctrinal concerns on the general church/denominational level: Episcopal Fund, General Administration Fund, World Service Fund, Ministerial Education Fund, and Interdenominational Cooperation Fund (our church has not contributed to this for two decades). Please note that 100% of apportioned amounts will be distributed/given/invested in bonafide United Methodist Ministries beyond Marietta First. None of these funds will be used in our local church ministry. By distributing these funds on a line item basis, we are maintaining our historic connection with The United Methodist Church, but exercising our stewardship responsibility not to support ministries which Christian conscience compel[s] us not to support, while at the same time supporting ministries which Christian conscience compel[s] us to support.Enclosure, Select Committee/jjd, Revised 3/23/98

D. Time line of actions subsequent to the apportionment withholding issue:

March 8, 1999. Letter to Bishop Lindsay Davis:

March 8, 1999
Bishop Lindsay Davis
North Georgia Conference
United Methodist Church
159 Ralph McGill Blvd., NE; Suite 208
Atlanta, GA 30308-3391

Dear Bishop Davis,
    I am writing you this letter with a broken heart. I find it inconceivable that you could make the decision that you have made

without the consideration of the congregation of the Marietta First United Methodist Church.

We spoke loudly at our Charge Conference and our Staff Parish Relations Committee has continued to speak to you regularly and with great conviction that moving of our pastor is not the desire of this body.

You made a statement that Charles Sineath is not an effective leader due to the apportionment withholding. Please understand, Bishop Davis, that Charles Sineath did not make this decision on his own. All he did was tell his congregation the truth. If more pastors and other leaders in the United Methodist Church would be so bold as to speak the truth about the happenings within this denomination, perhaps we could effect change. As it is, the Bishops threaten to move the pastors, or remove their credentials, threatening their livelihood and income as well as their careers if they so much as dare to tell their churches about what is going on "out there"; much less suggest any retributive action.

Do not be misled, Bishop Davis. This battle is not over. With the availability of the Internet and the easy accessibility of news and information from all over the country, more and more people are becoming informed and enlightened. The apostasy that has taken place in recent months in California and Illinois will not go unnoticed. The lack of action on the part of the Bishops and the heretical remarks on the part of some of these same Bishops will not go unpunished. Even though the United Methodist Church does not presently have in place any effective method for removing a Bishop from office, these actions most certainly will lead to the split of the denomination.

These issues are all about money and power. I see no reference to Godly leadership, to Christian discipleship, to spreading the gospel of Jesus Christ. The demand and seeking of money and power will ultimately lead to the demise of the United Methodist Church. God will surely judge all those in leadership harshly if they fail to speak truth and fail to attempt to lead others into the paths of righteousness.

God led me to this church, Marietta First United Methodist Church, not because it was Methodist but because He knew that the healing that I needed was available here. I came here a broken vessel in need of love and healing. I found it in the love, preaching, teaching, integrity, leadership and humility of my Senior Pastor, Charles Sineath. Mine is only one story. There are many hundreds, possibly thousands, of others, as I am sure you will hear.

Bishop Davis, I implore you to reconsider the stance you have taken. Do not punish this godly man for taking a stand for Jesus. Stand with us as we attempt to usher in renewal and revival to the honor and glory of the name that is shouted from the rooftops, Jesus Christ. If you are with us we can be the "voice heard around the world", if you attempt to squelch this statement of truth and faith, you will go down in history as the "Bishop who passed up his opportunity to be the Moses of United Methodism". We need a leader that will stand for truth, righteousness, integrity, and the gospel; Bishop Davis, do not let us down.

You have the ability, Bishop Davis, to turn this around; to use this for good. Be bold, courageous, and fearless in the face of the enemy, knowing that God is on the side of righteous.

In the Service of Jesus Christ,
[Original Signed by]
Ellen Beebe, Laity
Marietta First United Methodist Church
1255 Banberry Road
Marietta, GA 30067

Cc: Charles Sineath, Pastor
Bucky Smith, Chairman, Administrative Board
Jack Miller, Chairman, SPRC
Jamie Jenkins, District Superintendent

April 15, 1999. Transfer of Marietta minister seen by some as tied to dispute. Denomination leaders on Monday portrayed the transfer of the Rev. Charles Sineath, 22-year pastor of the 5,000-member First United Methodist Church of Marietta, as a routine personnel transfer. Sineath, who turns 60 this month, is five years from retirement. The announcement comes nearly a year after the church voted to withhold $58,427 in funds from the local conference over the national church's stands on social issues, including homosexuality. But the Rt. Rev. Lindsey Davis, bishop of the North Georgia Conference, said in a release that Sineath is just one of 50 ministers in the conference who will be reassigned this year. The Rev. Jamie Jenkins, superintendent of the Atlanta-Marietta district, has been involved in discussions with the church over the dispute, set off in 1997 when trustees at Methodist-founded Emory University agreed to permit same-sex commitment ceremonies at its campus chapels. The withholding of church funds from the local conference was about to come up again. One week ago, a group of staff and church members offered the conference all of this year's apportionment, if the bishop would agree to work on redirecting funds to programs the congregation endorsed. Robin Burruss, a lay leader of the church and a member of the Board of Stewards, said the compromise was rejected.... Burruss said the loss of the senior pastor after 21 years could have a serious impact on the church, which is in the middle of a $3 million expansion.

    - *The Atlanta Journal-Constitution*; By Tucker McQueen. Source: E-mail from Mr. Janz Mynderup.

April 15, 1999. Georgia church withholds funds amid talk of split. ATLANTA (UMNS) — The board of stewards of Marietta First United Methodist Church has voted to withhold all of the financial support that it typically provides at the conference and denominational levels, as some members talk openly about leaving the church and forming a new congregation. The 108-56 vote took place April 11 and applies to all of the "apportionment" dollars that have been requested of Marietta First by the larger church. Earlier this year, Bishop Lindsey Davis announced that the Rev. Charles Sineath, 60, would not be reappointed to Marietta First after 22 years. Since then Sineath has announced his plans to retire in June from the United Methodist ministry.

    The decision to withhold all apportionments, except the pastor's pension, was an expansion of an earlier decision by the board of stewards not to pay several "general church" funds that support the work of the church on the denominational level....The church's total apportionments for 1999 are $268,087. Previously the church had decided to withhold about $67,000 of that amount. [Board Chairman Bucky] Smith said the board had wanted to withhold all apportionments back in March 1998, when the apportionment debate surfaced for the first time. Then, the board voted to pay all of its conference support for 1998 but to "redirect" to conference causes the amount that would have gone to certain funds at the denominational level. "Only through Charles' leadership and the board's respect for him did we withhold only about 25-26 percent," Smith said. "Now that Charles has been taken out of the picture and is not being reappointed, the action reflects what the board wanted to do a year ago."....[People] in the church...believe the cabinet's decision to move Sineath was...punitive action. "The Methodist system is broken and corrupt," said church lay leader Robin Burruss, "and I don't think we should put a penny into a broken and corrupt system."...

Sineath has advocated the withholding of certain general church apportionments because "conscience compels us not to be part of what is displeasing to God." "We're not dealing with persnickety things," he said in an earlier interview. "We're dealing with issues we think are at the heart of our faith, the incarnation, the authority of Scripture, the blood atonement." ...A 38-page report compiled by a group within the church last year cites a number of incidents in which certain general agency executives and seminary professors are alleged to have questioned the deity of Jesus and the authority of Scripture, or to have espoused feminist theology or the acceptance of homosexuality. That report, however, does not address Emory University's decision to allow same-sex ceremonies under narrow circumstances, although that action keeps resurfacing in board discussions as a key reason for withholding apportionments. In 1997, Emory's board of trustees, which includes five United Methodist bishops [one of whom is Lindsay Davis of the North Georgia Conference], voted unanimously to allow same-sex ceremonies in the university chapel if the couple's faith permits it, and if the ceremony is conducted by a clergy person of that faith who has a direct tie to the university. But, Burruss says, the possibility of such a ceremony taking place at all "is contrary to Scripture and not the right thing."

- Internet, April 15, 1999; Nashville, Tennessee. 10-21-71B\{203\};
by Alice Smith, Executive Director of the Georgia UM Communications Council

April 27, 1999. "As of 1 A. M. EDT today, Charles (Sineath) has
been relieved of all responsibilities, by Mr. Davis [i.e., Bishop
Davis], as pastor of FUMC-Marietta. He is to clean out his office
and not return to the premises. The reason for this action is that he
is to be named tonight as the new pastor of a new church in
Marietta."
- Source: Internet, E-mail from B.J. Eble, former member of
FUMC Marietta, Georgia; April 27, 1999 12:31 PM
[Note: Reportedly, the following day, the locks were changed on
the doors so that Dr. Sineath could not get back into his offices.]

May - June, 1999. It is reported that the people from FUMC -
Marietta have been allowed to not pay any of their apportionments
this year. The reason projected is that approximately 80% of the
active members, to include many substantial contributors, have left
the church to form a new congregation.
- Source: Internet - E-mail from a former member of FUMC -
Marietta

June 1, 1999. Marietta church cuts staff. A month after several
hundred of its members met to form a new congregation, First
United Methodist Church [FUMC] of Marietta has reduced its staff
and budget. The church, which had a staff of about 45 and an annual budget of $3.3 million, cut 18 employees and $1 million from
its budget for the rest of the year....the congregational split is responsible for the cutbacks at First Marietta, which has a membership of about 5,300. About 650 adults and 150 children from First
United are meeting Tuesday nights as Wesleyan Fellowship, an
independent congregation with Methodist doctrine. First United
expects its membership to go down when Wesleyan Fellowship
begins officially accepting members....[FUMC] is the home congregation of Gov. Roy Barnes and U.S. Rep. Bob Barr. But Barr
said in a telephone interview last week he may be among those

leaving the church, where he married his current wife in 1986. "I don't feel comfortable staying with a particular church that penalizes its pastors for living by what they believe is the word of God," Barr said."God's blessed us—he really has," said Bucky Smith, former chairman of First United's board and an organizer of Wesleyan Fellowship. "The train's moving so fast, we can barely keep up."

- "Marietta church cuts staff," *The Atlanta Journal-Constitution*, June 1, 1999.

June 15, 1999. Report "Wesleyan Fellowship"; from the fledgling "Wesleyan Fellowship" that former members of FUMC - Marietta have started since Lindsey Davis ousted The Reverend Charles Sineath from that church (FUMC-M) is one of rapid growth. Below is a summary given by one of FUMC's former members via e-mail:

Date: Tue, 15 Jun 1999 19:43:19 GMT

Hey, Don, Wesleyan Fellowship is being blessed beyond our imagination; all information about the church is spread via word of mouth or internet.....here are some astonishing results:

* Decided on a Friday afternoon to have the 1st informational meeting on the next Tuesday night.....prepared for 200-300 folks.................OVER 700 ATTENDED.

* Decided that Tuesday June 22 would be the 1st service. Due to feedback started having services every Tuesday (but Charles could not speak) starting 5/18........Averaging over 650 adults, 120 youth, 40 nursery.

* Wanted strong youth ministry person and started search........Terry Tekyl had a vision of who the youth ministers would be and told them before they were asked and on 8/15 the 1st service for our youth with their two (!!!!!!!!!!) new youth leaders and their wives will take place.

* Wanted a facility to start Sunday services by 9/10.........Start Sunday Services this week!!!!

* Do not pass the offering plate at the services.......Have received over $150,000 in 5 gatherings/services.

209

* Needed office space.....had a company move out of Marietta and they gave their office space with 14 months pre-paid rent to the church.....with 5 offices......There will be 4 ministers and 1 secretary when everyone is on board!!

* Over 380 families have asked for membership, constituting over 1000 individuals. (and that number does not include many folks like myself who will be transferring membership after our youth camp 7/3-9)

The blessings continue at a rate so fast it's hard to keep up!!!!! I'll keep you posted on further developments.

- Source: e-mail from Mr. B. J. Eble, former member, FUMC Marietta.

August 3, 1999. From Ellen Beebe, member of the newly-formed Wesleyan Fellowship:

August 3, 1999

Dear Allen -

How can mere words express "how I'm doing"?

I am mature enough to know that there will be down days...that everything will not always go exactly like I wish it would...however, currently I am living in a "goosebump" world! God is performing miracle after miracle, right before our eyes! I am also learning what God means when He tells us that He knows what is best for us and that we must trust Him.

We are praying as we never have before. We are worshiping as if we just discovered that worship was possible. We live for Sundays, when we all come together as a Christian Community. People are arriving 1- 1 1/2 hours early and staying 1- 2 hours late! It's like a wonderful family reunion every time we come together.

The Sunday School classes are continuing to meet, in homes, in clubhouses, in old offices, wherever room can be found. Bonds are deepening, ties are tightening, trust is building, the groundwork is being laid. When we are ready to structure the small/cell groups we will be ready.

210

It was suggested that we all read "Reap the Harvest" by Joel Comisky, a book about cell groups/churches. Two Sundays in a row, a case of books has been brought in, only to be sold out in minutes. People are hungry, they are thirsty, we are preparing ourselves to be the body that God desires for us to be.

God is so good. Words cannot express. We are being the church. Do you know what I mean? We are anointing one another with oil, we are praying with conviction for healing, we are daring to go the elders and ask for prayer. People are praying Acts 2:42. People are studying the books of Acts. Asking God to grant them insight into what the church is supposed to look and act like.

We are not passing an offering plate. We have merely stationed a chest and buckets at the doors. An announcement is made that they are there should anyone desire to give. Needless to say, the offerings are incredible! When people are not coerced into giving, made to feel guilty if they can't give to every offering that comes up on top of their tithe, they find money to throw into the pot! Freely and cheerfully!

My friends and I have shared stories about how our daily lives are changing. We find ourselves doing spontaneous acts of charity. Giving money to the homeless, instead of avoiding them. Looking for ways to do random acts of kindness.

Friends are telling me of new desires to study God's word. To do Bible studies, such as Experiencing God.

God is drawing us close and we are running to keep up! It is so good that I want to share it with everyone! We have begun to pray that the lost would just show up..be drawn in by the Holy Spirit so that we could share with them, show them what the church is supposed to be like! Love on them!

It's wonderful.

Yes, you may share this letter in any way you wish. Tell the world that church can be fun, that obedience is fulfilling, that worship is greater than you could ever imagine it to be. That God loves His children and desires to draw them close and love on them so that He can prepare them to serve Him!

In His Service,

Ellen Beebe

- Source: E-mail from "Ellen Beebe, Laity, Wesleyan Fellowship; LN4Prayer@aol.com; Tue Aug 03 09:12:12 1999"

Appendix T

Case Study: Camp Ground United Methodist Church (CGUMC)
Fayetteville, North Carolina

This case study describes retaliatory action taken for assisting members of another congregation to resist pro-lesbian advocacy in their church, and associated events. More complete details are avaialable on the Concerned Methodists website.

March 6 - May 17, 1994. At a Finance Committee meeting in the CGUMC fellowship hall, Rev. George Jones alleged that financial information supplied by Concerned Methodists (CM) was not true; my response was, "Oh yes it is too!" Rev. Jones' face turned red. Afterwards, in a private conversation I told him, "I know that the district superintendent [DS] (Tommy Smith) and the bishop are putting pressure on you because of what we (i.e., CM) are doing, but don't get involved in this."

March 6, 1994. At the Council on Ministries (COM) meeting I had requested time to discuss the problem of the heresy at the Re-Imagining Conference (RC) that had been promoted in Nov. 1993. (I had sent COM Chair Charlie Astrike a letter of concern the RC.) He said, "I'll give you one minute to talk about it!" After I had raised the issue, Rev. Jones explained it away with "There weren't that many people who attended"; "It's a dead issue"; and "How do you know? You weren't there.". [Despite the fact that since that time Charlie has repeatedly been given copies of my original letter, he has yet to respond.]

On or about August 6, 1994. Date of a meeting held at CGUMC while I was on travel which sought to counter questions I had raised about the RC. One attendee told me that Rev. Jones had told the people, "I'll give you five minutes to tell me about your concerns about the RC"; it was then that she leaned over and told another member, "Wouldn't you know it; they wait until Al [Morris] is gone to discuss this."

November 6, 1994 at 4:35 P.M. I arrived at CGUMC) to attend the Youth Council meeting. Rev. Jones told me that he needed to talk to me in his office. He told me that I had gone out and torn up the church at Ocracoke. I replied that what he had said was not the truth, that those people had requested my assistance to oppose a pastor who was attempting to push lesbianism. George then said that if I didn't resign as a youth director, he would bring the action before the Administrative Board (Ad. Board) to have me removed. I told him that if it weren't for the kids, I would be glad to fight it, but to not cause any disruption, I would. That evening, I told Mrs. Barbara Poole that I would be resigning; she evidently knew that I would be asked to resign since she was visibly upset with tears in her eyes. She stated, "I just cannot take pressure." She hugged me and asked me if I wanted talk to the kids? I declined because, again, I didn't want to upset them.

A few nights later, I called Mrs. Kathy O' Neal, narrated what had happened, and asked her if I had done anything to disrupt their Charge Conference. She was adamant in that I had not, and asked, "How can they say that? That has nothing to do with the truth!" In a call to her later, she stated that she, Mr. & Mrs. Fletcher C. Hoggard, and others would be willing to drive to Fayetteville to speak on my behalf. I told her that it would not be necessary to do that.

November 22, 1994. Date of letter from George Jones that stated my request for a hearing before the Ad. Board [made via a letter] would not be granted, in addition to "I know that you have also harmed the life of the little UMC at Ocracoke very seriously for such a small church cannot bear the pain you brought to bear with your negativity and dissension. I also know that I have had several parents question why you were working with the youth group...It is simply too negative of an example." [Note: The allegation of the anonymous parents was similar to one used when George attempted to pull the same tactic on another member of the church - Sandy Holland. In that situation, he alleged that "some people" objected to how Sandy was fulfilling her duties. When Sandy asked for the names, George refused to tell her. Later, Sandy's husband Bill went into George's office and told him that there would be no more instances of George calling Sandy into his office and stated that until he (George) told the names of these anonymous "people" he (Bill) would assume that they did not exist.]

November 23, 1994. I received a letter from the people at Ocracoke dated November the 20th containing the signatures of 27 people attesting to the fact that I had not caused the disruption at their church.

November 28, 1994. Terry Preiss told me that in a phone conversation with Rev. Jones, he had told Terry that he (Jones) was getting pressure from the DS and Bishop C. P. Minnick to remove me from the Youth Program for "tearing up the church out at Ocracoke" and words to the effect that "They're putting pressure on me...I have to do something!"

November 29, 1994. I received a second letter (dated November 28th) from Rev. Jones containing false allegations that I had called people and attempted to convince them to leave the church. Jimmy R. Cash, Sr. received a letter from him similar to the one I had. Jimmy immediately called the DS's office and mentioned the possibility of legal action; Rev. Jones quickly called Jimmy Cash back, apologized, and told Jimmy, "I've got to do something about Al. The DS and bishop are putting pressure on me."

December, 1994. I received information that Bishop Minnick was heard to say that he was going to force me out of the United Methodist Church. Believing this to be reliable information, I consulted an attorney.

January 8, 1995. Rev. Jones stated to the Administrative Board (Ad. Board) that he had removed me from my position as counselor because I did not present a good example to the youth. He then asked for a motion to be made; this was done by John Smith and seconded by Robert Smith. The chair of the Ad. Board, Jay Spillane, called for a vote and declared the motion passed with no call for discussion, nor giving me an opportunity to defend myself since I was not a member of the Board. The motion passed without one example of misconduct being cited by Rev. Jones (nor could he).

February, 1995. From a confidential source, I was given to understand that Bishop Minnick had given Rev. Jones instructions before he was assigned to CGUMC to "force me out of the church" or words to that effect.

November 20, 1995. Meeting with Rev. Jones in the office of the DS (Rev. Tommy Smith) in an attempt to arrive at a reconciliation. During the course of the conversation, I expressed the opinion that I believed Rev. Jones "stacked" boards with his own people so as to get a favorable decision on whatever he proposed, especially the Ad. Board and the PPR. I further told him that I had called two friends I had who were members of the clergy in the North Carolina Conference to verify my perceptions, and they had told me that this was "common practice" in the UMC. Jimmy Cash reinforced this with the observation that a study by a prominent Methodist scholar writing in Christianity Today magazine showed that this was commonly done in the UMC. Reverend Smith then said, "Who was that pastor? I won't tolerate that practice!" He expressed outrage. I told him that Concerned Methodists had a strict policy of keeping conversations with UM clergy confidential. At another point in the meeting when we were discussing the points made in Rev. Jones' letters of November 22, 1994 and November 28, 1994, I had made the point that what was contained in them was not the truth. Rev. Jones refused to acknowledge it and attempted to change the subject. I then told him, "No, George. That's the only thing on the table right now. When you said that, that was a lie!" He again attempted to change the subject, and I again told him, "No, George. That's the only thing on the table. When you said that, that was a lie!" I then offered him the opportunity to apologize to me for the lies contained in the letters dated November 22 and November 28, 1994. This too he refused to do. The meeting ended with nothing having been resolved.

April 6, 1996. Jimmy Cash said that on April third Rev. Lloyd Willis told him in the presence of Julia Willis (no relation to Rev. Willis) that Rev. Smith was furious that he (Willis) had let Jimmy back into the UMC. Rev. Smith then told Rev. Willis, "Well, don't put him in any leadership positions or put him on any boards." He also took issue with Rev. Willis for letting me preach. Rev. Willis asked, "Well, what was wrong with that? He gave his testimony and it was well received." Marty Rasmussen later told me that he had been informed by two of his pastors that Rev. Smith had requested he be removed from his position as church treasurer because of his association with Concerned Methodists. On another occasion, Rev. Willis said that he was in Rev. Smith's office talking to him when one of the certified letters from Concerned Methodists arrived. Rev. Smith interrupted the conversation, picked up the telephone, called Rev. Jones and said, "Get over here right now!"

November 18, 1996. Date of a letter from Rev. Jones to Bud Harrub, pastor of FUMC, Mt. Pleasant, TN. It said in part, "The Administrative Board voted to start proceedings to expel him [i.e., me] but did not follow through due to my recommendations." [This was later shown to be a false statement.]

December 6, 1996. Date of letters to Sally Smith and Roger Carroll (former and present chairs of PPR), and John Smith and Joseph Spillane (former and present chairs of Ad. Board) requesting background information on what Rev. Jones had sent to Bud Harrub about the "proceedings to expel" me from the UMC. No answer was ever received from any of these four individuals, with the exception of Roger Carroll.

December 18, 1996. My letter to Bishop Marion Edwards requesting help in receiving answers from Smith, Carroll, Smith, and

Spillane. No answer was ever received from Bishop Edwards to this request for information.

January 27, 1997; 9:20 P.M. I attempted to get Barbara Poole discuss with me about what she had allegedly told others about my work with the youth. She screamed, "I'm not going to talk with you about it."

January 28 and February 11, 1997. Dates of letters to Barbara Poole requesting that she meet and talk with me about the information she had allegedly communicated to others about my work with the youth.

March 3, 1997. Letter from Bishop Edwards to me stating that my complaint was based on "major disagreements" with...George Jones.

March 14, 1997. My letter to Bishop Edwards requesting he reconsider his decision to dismiss my complaints against George Jones: "It is difficult for me to understand how clearly identifiable instances of lying can be attributed to 'major disagreement.'"...

June 1997. George Jones was reappointed to Camp Ground Church. Some of the long-time members left, vowing not to return until he was gone.

July 25, 1998. I called Steve Thomas in accordance with Matthew 5:23, 24; and Matthew 18:15. I requested to speak with him; he refused. I again requested it; he again refused.
********************End of Statement********************

The above timeline statement is true and correct to the best of my knowledge. I used a running chronology of events, notes, memoranda for record, and exhibits used as evidence supporting the charges I had filed against Rev. Jones for lying; much more happened than is contained here.

It should be stated that I have no animosity for anyone involved in this. I am saddened that George would have engaged in the actions he did. I am also sorry that some of the laity in my own church would have let themselves be used as they were; they did not think for themselves. I am personally embarrassed to mention some of these events, but believe it to be necessary so that others will know that when similar actions happen to them, these are not isolated cases.

This case study illustrates several phenomena, that of retaliatory action against me for my assisting the members of OUMC fight (and win) the battle to save their church. In addition, it shows several tactics that are commonly used by what we call "Company Men" to effect their will in a local church: the co-opting of lay members, fabrication of charges, working behind the scenes, demonization, etc. When I attempted to get basic information on being "kicked out of the church" (again, which was shown to be a lie), I met a wall of silence from four people, three of whom had had kids in the youth program while I had been the Youth Coordinator and a youth counselor. (Over the space of 14 years, I have worked with over 200 youth in two churches and an orphanage in Korea, received many compliments, and maintained my life above reproach.) Such was the influence that George Jones had on some of the members of our church. However, his actions caught up with him and, during his tenure at our church, many folks departed - often to other denominations. One person remarked, "The people who left is like a 'Who's Who' of the leading members of Camp Ground." Such is the damage that can be done to a local church - when people let it happen.

- Allen O. Morris, Member, Camp Ground Church